JOURNALISM
UNDER FIRE

COLUMBIA JOURNALISM REVIEW BOOKS

COLUMBIA JOURNALISM REVIEW BOOKS

For more than fifty years, the *Columbia Journalism Review* has been the gold standard for media criticism, holding the profession to the highest standards and exploring where journalism is headed, for good and for ill.

Columbia Journalism Review Books expands upon this mission, seeking to publish titles that allow for greater depth in exploring key issues confronting journalism, both past and present, and pointing to new ways of thinking about the field's impact and potential.

Drawing on the expertise of the editorial staff at the *Columbia Journalism Review* as well as the Columbia Journalism School, the series of books will seek out innovative voices and reclaim important works, traditions, and standards. In doing this, the series will also incorporate new ways of publishing made available by the Web and e-books.

JOURNALISM UNDER FIRE

PROTECTING THE FUTURE OF INVESTIGATIVE REPORTING

STEPHEN GILLERS

Columbia University Press   *New York*

Columbia University Press
Publishers Since 1893
New York   Chichester, West Sussex
cup.columbia.edu

Library of Congress Cataloging-in-Publication Data
Names: Gillers, Stephen, 1943– author.
Title: Journalism under fire : protecting the future of
investigative reporting / Stephen Gillers.
Description: New York : Columbia University Press, 2018. |
Series: Columbia journalism review of books |
Includes bibliographical references and index.
Identifiers: LCCN 2017058610 (print) | LCCN 2018000758 (ebook) |
ISBN 9780231547338 (e-book) | ISBN 9780231168861 (cloth : alk. paper)
| ISBN 9780231168878 (pbk. : alk. paper)
Subjects: LCSH: Reporters and reporting—
Law and legislation—United States.
Classification: LCC KF2750 (ebook) | LCC KF2750 .G55 2018 (print)
| DDC 342.7308/53—dc23
LC record available at https://lccn.loc.gov/2017058610

Columbia University Press books are printed on permanent
and durable acid-free paper.
Printed in the United States of America

Cover design: Milenda Nan Ok Lee

Cover image: Everett Collection Inc. / © Alamy

For Barbara S. Gillers

CONTENTS

ACKNOWLEDGMENTS

Close by, I had guidance from two lawyers and a journalist: Barbara S. Gillers, Gillian Gillers, and Heather Gillers, respectively. I thank Steven Shapiro and Burt Neuborne for reading portions of the book and offering advice. I am grateful to Lindsey E. Smith, JD, NYU School of Law 2018, for proofreading the manuscript and checking citations with spectacular attention to detail. I benefited from presenting some of my arguments to journalism and law faculty at the University of Missouri. I also thank the D'Agostino/Greenberg Fund for financial assistance that enabled me to work on this book. Victor Navaksy had the idea for this book, although I cannot promise that the book as published is exactly, or even roughly, what had he had in mind. But it would not have been written without his late-night call a couple of years ago.

JOURNALISM
UNDER FIRE

INTRODUCTION

My subject is freedom of the press generally and investigative journalism in particular. My argument is built on two premises. First, a free press is essential to American democracy. Until recently, this premise would have seemed self-evident. Today, it may be quixotic. President Trump's incessant hostility to journalism and the nearly daily attacks on "fake news," including a charge from within the White House that the press is "the enemy of the people," can only encourage the public's already declining trust in the news. That the White House offers no evidence to support its accusations seems irrelevant. Whether a fact is true or false seems for many to have become a political question, not an empirical one. That view is unlikely to disappear with the end of the Trump presidency. So it may not seem an opportune time to write a book arguing to expand press freedom. I suggest, however, that the improbability of even modest success at this moment is precisely why the effort is necessary. Legal scholars, historians, students of government and journalism, and, most important, the press must respond forcefully to public and private efforts to demean journalism and to disparage its importance to democracy.

They may lose in the short run. They may even lose in the long run. But they must resist the assault in the belief and hope that they will win in the end.

My second premise is that because the First Amendment, legislation, and court opinions are the primary sources of press freedom, the meaning of freedom of the press in the United States must begin with what the law *now* says. "Now" is the key word. Law is the necessary starting point only because law is where freedoms are formally recognized or denied. But the law on press freedom is no more than an expression of public policy in another form. We must begin with law but not end there. The broader public-policy question is more prescriptive than descriptive: it asks what freedom of the press *should* be in order best to serve democracy, not simply what courts happen to say about it at the moment. The law can change, and has changed, to respond to the questions.

There is freedom *to* and freedom *from*. How much of each should the law give the press? And how should it do so? Those are among the questions that this book will try to answer. Answers must begin with the Constitution. Congress, the First Amendment tells us, "shall make no law . . . abridging the freedom of . . . the press." This is the Press Clause. What does it mean? The Supreme Court once treated it as a source of rights for an institution called the press, and it should do so again. The Press Clause should be interpreted to recognize the importance of journalists to the American system of government and to democracy. Lately, however, the Press Clause has been mostly missing from Supreme Court opinions and public discussion. Certainly, we hear the phrase "freedom of the press" often enough, but outside the legal academy, we hear little specifically about the Press Clause.

An argument that the Press Clause should be seen as an independent source of rights for something called the press or someone called a journalist—rights in addition to those the Constitution elsewhere guarantees to everyone—will require answering many questions. Preliminarily, there is the matter of framer intent. What did those who wrote the First Amendment intend when they said that press freedom could not be abridged? After answering that question, to the extent we can and need to do so, we must turn to two others: First, what can we learn about the meaning of the Press Clause solely from the text of the First Amendment? Second, how has the Supreme Court construed the Press Clause over time, and what is the Court's position today? These two questions form the core of chapter 1.

Disregarding precedent, and at times disingenuously, the Supreme Court has in recent decades ignored the Press Clause. Why? A partial answer seems to be that the Court does not know how to define the press without including everyone who offers information to the public. In an earlier era, we might have said that the press was the institutional press— newspapers, magazines, and the broadcast news. That definition, while imperfect, was fairly easy to apply. But it excluded those who do what journalists do yet lack an institutional affiliation or who today may be affiliated with organizations other than the legacy media. This is where matters get especially complicated. Because today technology permits nearly anyone to claim to be a journalist—if a journalist is defined as anyone who offers information to the general public or a segment of it—why do we need the Press Clause at all? Its First Amendment cousin, the Speech Clause, can protect all freedom of expression. We would not need to define a subset of information providers called journalists. That, in fact, is the unfortunate path that the Supreme Court seems to have chosen. While the Court routinely includes both the Speech and Press Clauses when it quotes the First Amendment, the Press Clause has been eclipsed as a distinct source of rights available only to the press. The press becomes just another speaker. So the Speech Clause, which forbids abridging freedom of speech, has been seen to suffice. As my colleague Burt Neuborne has written, the Supreme Court has given the "Free Press Clause virtually no independent meaning. The Court reads it as a colony of an imperial Free Speech Clause that does all the heavy legal lifting. If the Free Press Clause is mentioned at all, it's usually to reject a separate role for it."[1]

I will argue that the Press Clause contains a distinct set of rights for the press that the Constitution does not give all speakers. That claim requires a definition of the press. I reject the well-intentioned but dangerous proposition that today technology enables everyone to be a journalist. That view consigns the Press Clause to oblivion. If, constitutionally, everyone can be the press, there is no press. But if there is a press, who or what qualifies? What makes the press different from other speakers? And what do we expect from the press in exchange for the added protections the Press Clause guarantees against abridgment by Congress and the states? No argument in favor of a robust Press Clause will succeed unless the press offers something in return. That something is what makes it the press. In chapters 2 and 3, I will argue that a vital Press Clause requires the exercise of editorial judgment and judicial deference (but not abdication) to that judgment. As one federal appeals court wrote in dismissing a libel claim against *Newsweek*:

Courts must be slow to intrude into the area of editorial judgment, not only with respect to choices of words, but also with respect to inclusions in or omissions from news stories. Accounts of past events are always selective, and under the First Amendment the decision of what to select must almost always be left to writers and editors. It is not the business of government.[2]

If we accept an independent role for the Press Clause, generally agree on a definition of the press and how we resolve claims to press status if disputed, and describe what the press owes democracy in exchange for heightened constitutional freedom, we must next define the content of that freedom. That content is the focus of chapters 4 and 5, whose subjects are legal protections for, respectively, a reporter's sources and newsgathering. It would hardly be worth going through the preliminary inquiries unless there is a Press Clause payoff that benefits democracy. An overlooked 1991 dissenting opinion by Justice Souter, in which Justices Marshall, Blackmun, and O'Connor joined, and a 2001 concurring opinion by Justice Breyer, joined by Justice O'Connor, provide the intellectual framework for a Press Clause jurisprudence that can protect sources and newsgathering.

The Press Clause rights described in chapters 4 and 5 are not meant to be exclusive. The meaning of the Press Clause is not (and never has been) static. As new circumstances arise, its meaning may change and its protections expand, as has been true for the Constitution's Speech Clause, Due Process Clause, Equal Protection Clause, and other provisions of the Bill of Rights.

The special concern of this book is protection for investigative reporting. Investigative reporting is essential to the work of our democracy. Richard Tofel, president of Pro-Publica, has offered a particularly good definition, suitable here.

> The best definition of what constitutes "investigative" journalism, at least in this author's experience, is journalism that seeks to reveal something that someone with some modicum of power (a person, group or institution) seeks to keep a secret. In this respect, investigative journalism is unlike most reporting, which announces, transmits or explicates something which someone (whether powerful or powerless) is seeking straightforwardly and transparently to have disseminated—from public meetings and political campaigns to financial and commodities markets, to news conferences, press releases and promotional events of all kinds, to cultural, entertainment or sporting events.[3]

I would expand Tofel's definition to make explicit what is implicit. It is not *any* secret that investigative reporters seek to reveal but rather secrets that conceal abuses of power, threats to democratic institutions, and dangers to the lives, health, safety, freedoms, or livelihoods of others by private or public actors. People have always been willing to harm or tolerate harm to others, even countless others, to increase their wealth, fame, and power. We know to expect it. Investigative journalism is an essential antidote. It is not the only one, of course. Courts, law-enforcement agencies, the executive and legislative branches of government, and the private bar are among the others. But journalists can do things that others cannot or will not do or have just overlooked.

Experience tells us that there are people with wealth and power who are willing to tolerate harm to democratic institutions and to others and lie about it in order to (further) enrich or empower themselves. For advancement or recognition or because they are bribed or incompetent, public officials may do the same or tolerate it. History has many examples. A glance at some winners of the Pulitzer Prize for investigative reporting should erase any doubt.[4]

2017: Eric Eyre, *Charleston Gazette-Mail*, Charleston, West Virginia, for courageous reporting, performed in the face of powerful opposition, to expose the flood of opioids flowing into depressed West Virginia counties with the highest overdose death rates in the country.

2014: Chris Hamby, Center for Public Integrity, Washington, DC, for his reports on how some lawyers and doctors rigged a system to deny benefits to coal miners stricken with black lung disease, resulting in remedial legislative efforts.

2010: Barbara Laker and Wendy Ruderman, *Philadelphia Daily News*, for their resourceful reporting that exposed a rogue police narcotics squad, resulting in an FBI probe and the review of hundreds of criminal cases tainted by the scandal.

2009: David Barstow, *New York Times*, for his tenacious reporting that revealed how some retired generals, working as radio and television analysts, had been co-opted by the Pentagon to make its case for the war in Iraq, and how many of them also had undisclosed ties to companies that benefited from policies they defended.

2007: Brett Blackledge, *Birmingham News* (Alabama), for his exposure of cronyism and corruption in the state's two-year college system, resulting in the dismissal of the chancellor and other corrective action.

2001: David Willman, *Los Angeles Times*, for his pioneering exposé of seven unsafe prescription drugs that had been approved by the Food and Drug Administration and an analysis of the policy reforms that had reduced the agency's effectiveness.

Beyond the Press Clause, chapter 6 urges legislation to protect and enable investigative reporting. It proposes a publicly endowed Fund for Investigative Journalism, much like the endowments that support the arts and the humanities. We cannot yet know the full effect of the internet on the finances of news organizations, but we do know that it has caused and will continue to cause changes in the traditional business model. Whether a news organization is for-profit or not-for-profit; whether it is solely web based or also publishes on paper; whether its coverage is local, national, or international; and however it views its mission, it must pay its bills. There are four obvious ways it can do so: reader subscriptions, newsstand sales, advertising, and donations. Chapter 6 proposes a fifth way—government funding accompanied by mechanisms to ensure independence.

Also in chapter 6 are three other recommendations. The first would make freedom-of-information acts more responsive to media inquiries and less costly to enforce judicially. The second recommendation advocates a federal anti-SLAPP statute. None now exists. SLAPP is an acronym for "strategic lawsuits against public participation." A wealthy plaintiff (or his moneyed sympathizers) can inflict great financial harm on a press institution or a journalist simply by suing. The plaintiff or his funder may not especially care about winning. For some plaintiffs, the prospect of court victory may not be primary. Instead, the goal may be to force the defendant to spend both time and money by making the court fight as prolonged and expensive as possible. State anti-SLAPP laws aim to frustrate this strategy and, more broadly, protect the press whatever may be the plaintiff's motives. They enable defendants (including the press) who are sued because of something they wrote or said to get a speedy judicial ruling on the validity of the plaintiff's claim against them, thereby saving time and legal and expert-witness fees, and if the case is dismissed, to recoup those fees from the plaintiff. Nearly half the states have no anti-SLAPP law, and the laws in some states that do have one are weak. A federal anti-SLAPP law will correct this. The final recommendation will protect the right to appeal.

The proposals in this book are structural. They aim to build a protected space where journalists can work shielded from those who may seek to impede them either by interfering with their ability to discover facts or by suing (or prosecuting) them for what they report. The proposals here would be ambitious in the best of times. Today, they are fanciful. Certainly that is so for the proposals that require federal legislation. Prospects for legislation will be better in some states. Other proposals—for the protection of confidential sources and for newsgathering—can be judicially accomplished through interpretation of the Press Clause. I don't say that

these goals will have an easier time in the courts than in legislatures, only that the decision makers will be judges, not
politicians.

The best way to contest efforts to weaken the press is for
the press to do its job professionally, one day at a time. It must
labor to report the truth in the optimistic belief—obligatory
even at the darkest moments—that doing so matters. Attacks
on the integrity of the press cannot be stopped. The First
Amendment protects the critics. But the attacks can be rebut-
ted through persistence and good work.

Work on this book started in the year that *Spotlight* won
the Academy Award for best picture. The film tells how the
Boston Globe's investigative team exposed pedophilia by Cath-
olic priests in Massachusetts and how the church tried to
suppress disclosure of the abuse. The *Globe*'s reporting
inspired other journalists to investigate the same misconduct
elsewhere in the United States and abroad. The film will
interest a new generation of college students in careers in
journalism, just as Carl Bernstein and Bob Woodward did
four decades earlier in their Watergate reporting, memorialized in the film *All the President's Men*. There will be much
work for the next generation of journalists to do. There is
much responsibility on the rest of us, the beneficiaries of that
work, to make it possible for them to do it. The questions
here are too important to leave in the sole care of courts and
lawyers.

1

WHAT DOES THE PRESS
CLAUSE MEAN?

The First Amendment says: "Congress shall make no law . . . abridging the freedom of speech or of the press." This statement contains a Speech Clause and a Press Clause. What does the Press Clause add to the Speech Clause? Much turns on the answer. Today, the Supreme Court treats the First Amendment's Press Clause as constitutionally redundant, leaving the Speech Clause to do the work of protecting oral and written expression. As Sonja West has written:

> What does the Press Clause mean, and does it differ from the Speech Clause? On a purely textual basis, the answers to these questions seem clear—it means something, and it is different. Yet somehow, over time, this promising provision has devolved into nothing more than constitutional window dressing. The Court's modern practice of reading the First Amendment with its judicial thumb over the Press Clause has led to wide acceptance that the Press Clause has become "redundant and thus irrelevant."[1]

Although the Court has rarely been enthusiastic about developing a robust Press Clause jurisprudence, decades ago it viewed the clause as a distinct source of rights for an institution called the press. The Court once seemed to know what "the press" was and why it was constitutionally important to protect it. Today, it appears largely to have forgotten. The need now is for a revival of the Press Clause and an expansive interpretation of the freedoms it guarantees. Democracy demands revival and expansion in order for the press to do its job. That job requires (among other things) that the press be able to report on threats posed by three overlapping social and political trends that concentrate power, and therefore the potential for the abuse of power, and that show no signs of abating. These are the increasing influence of money in politics; the increasing concentration of individual and corporate wealth, which contributes to and benefits from the first trend; and the increasing ability of government and private actors to use technology to collect and store vast amounts of information about people without their knowledge, which is a threat to privacy and therefore freedom.

THE INFLUENCE OF FRAMER INTENT

The framers' intended meaning of the Press Clause should not bind us, assuming we could know it and that all (or a majority) agreed. Law professors and historians have long debated the question. Because the scholarly debates are peripheral to the arguments here, and because the original intent is obscure, diving deeply into the academic literature would not be productive. An example should suffice. David Anderson, a leading scholar of the First Amendment, has argued for a broad reading of the framers' intent.

Though scholars today may debate whether the press clause has any significance independent of the speech clause, historically there is no doubt that it did. Freedom of the press—not freedom of speech—was the primary concern of the generation that wrote the Declaration of Independence, the Constitution, and the Bill of Rights. Freedom of speech was a late addition to the pantheon of rights; freedom of the press occupied a central position from the very beginning.[2]

Anderson challenged the narrow view of Leonard Levy, who argued in his influential 1960 book *Legacy of Suppression*[3] that the Press Clause was intended to prohibit prior restraints on (i.e., an injunction forbidding) publication and nothing more.[4] Levy partly retreated from this view later, but not so far as to agree with Anderson or other critics. Reviewing Levy's 1985 book *Emergence of a Free Press*,[5] Anderson wrote:

> In *Legacy*, the argument was that the press clause must have been intended only to prohibit prior restraints because no broader understanding was available when it was framed. But now Levy is forced to recognize that broader understandings were available—for example, that the framers realized popular government could not operate successfully unless the press was free to criticize officeholders and candidates.[6]

For my purposes, this may be a debate about little. Yet it is not about nothing. It is important because history is important. So framer intent is relevant to the argument here as one ingredient among many. But the original meaning of the Press Clause is not the final meaning. There is no final meaning. The framers did not expect that their intended meaning would be the meaning always, as Levy eventually acknowledged. He wrote that the "principles—not the Framers' understanding and applications of them—were meant to endure." And he added:

> The first amendment's injunction, that there shall be no law abridging the freedom of speech or press, was boldly stated if narrowly understood. The bold statement, not the narrow understanding, was written into the fundamental law. There is no evidence to warrant the belief, nor is there valid cause or need to believe, that the Framers possessed the ultimate wisdom and best insights on the meaning of freedom of expression. But what the first amendment said is far more important than what its Framers meant. It is enough that they gave constitutional recognition to the principle of freedom of speech and press in unqualified and undefined terms.[7]

Academic arguments over what the framers meant are academic in a second sense. As we will see, the Supreme Court has recognized the murkiness of the constitutional history. It has interpreted the First Amendment, including the Press Clause, unconstrained by any need to exhume and adhere to framer intent.

A further reason to refuse to shackle ourselves to framer intent is that the press of today is not the press of 1789. As Anderson has written:

> What history shows is that journalism has changed, conceptions of press have changed, and judicial (and perhaps popular) enthusiasm for protecting the press has waxed

and waned. Whatever "press" might mean today will necessarily be quite different from what it meant to the Framers, and probably from what it has meant at other times since then. The issue here is not whether history proves that press means journalism, but whether journalism might provide a satisfactory—if changing—conception of press. It can do so only if journalism can be distinguished from other types of information businesses.[8]

This freedom to develop the "principle of freedom of speech and press" allows the courts (and Congress through legislation) to serve the needs of the United States in the twenty-first century. Whether we do this through constitutional interpretation or legislation is secondary. The task is to do it in a way that protects the many jobs the press performs in our constitutional democracy. Two are my focus here: investigative reporting, which can depend on finding and interpreting often obscure and (sometimes) seemingly unconnected information, much of it publicly available; and publication of stories based on disclosures (or leaks) from unauthorized sources whose information is newsworthy, who will not speak for attribution, and whose disclosures may be unlawful.

I realize that the phrase "investigative reporting" (or synonyms) is not precise, but precision is not needed. In the introduction to this book, I quoted a definition by ProPublica's Richard Tofel, which works well for my purposes. We can add Justice Stewart's vision of the press as "a fourth institution outside the Government" that would provide "an additional check on the three official branches."[9] Many years ago, Vincent Blasi famously described the "checking" function of the press.[10] Whom does the watchdog watch, the checker check? The target is usually described as the government, but it is larger than that. Leonard Downie Jr. and Michael Schudson define the watchdog function this way:

> Independent reporting not only reveals what government or private interests appear to be doing but also what lies behind their actions. This is the watchdog function of the press—reporting that holds government officials accountable to the legal and moral standards of public service and keeps business and professional leaders accountable to society's expectations of integrity and fairness.[11]

Investigative stories tend to be long, deeply reported, and expensive to produce, so one impediment to the press's watchdog role is financial. The remedy is to address the cost. Another problem can be the difficulty in getting the information the story requires. This difficulty also has solutions—or, more accurately, ways to reduce the difficulty.[12]

THE PRESS CLAUSE:
A TEXTUAL ANALYSIS

The language of the First Amendment is where we must start:

> Congress shall make no law respecting an establishment of religion, or prohibiting the free exercise thereof; or abridging the freedom of speech, or of the press; or the right of the people peaceably to assemble, and to petition the Government for a redress of grievances.

Take the phrase "or abridging the freedom of speech, or of the press," and momentarily put aside how courts have interpreted these words. Focus on the text. We must read it to include the italicized words: "Congress shall make no law . . . abridging the freedom of speech, or *abridging the freedom* of the press." The framers, masters of brevity, did not repeat words that were necessarily implied. The words "abridging the freedom" are necessarily implied before "of the press." The word "abridging" is also necessarily implied before "the right . . . to assemble . . . and to petition." "The freedom of" is not needed there because the framers chose "the right . . . to" over "the freedom of." The punctuation supports this reading. There are commas after "religion," "speech," and "assemble" but semicolons after "thereof" and "press."

With the necessarily implied language, the amendment reads (additions in italics):

> Congress shall make no law respecting an establishment of religion, or prohibiting the free exercise thereof; or abridging the freedom of speech, or *abridging the freedom* of the press; or *abridging* the right of the people peaceably to assemble, and to petition the Government for a redress of grievances.

So much should be easy. But we are left with two textual questions. How we choose to answer them matters a great deal.

The first textual question asks whether the freedoms that the Press Clause protects against abridgment by Congress (and therefore the states)[13] are identical to the freedoms the Speech Clause protects. If so, "or of the Press" is redundant, which would be odd in a document so carefully drafted and debated. The Court itself has repeatedly emphasized that it will not assume redundancy in a statute.[14] Constitutions are written more carefully because it is harder to amend a constitution—certainly ours—than to repeal a statute.

The notion that the Press Clause is redundant of the Speech Clause is constitutionally unworthy. Engage in a short thought experiment. Imagine that the Press Clause appeared in a separate *sentence* in the First Amendment. Imagine, for example, that the amendment read: "Congress shall make no law . . . abridging the freedom of speech . . . the right to assemble . . . and to petition. . . . Nor shall Congress make any law abridging the freedom of the press." Or imagine an entirely separate *amendment* in the Bill of Rights that prohibited abridgment of press freedom. Redundancy could not in either instance plausibly be argued. The framers would then be said to have added a separate sentence or a separate amendment that carried no independent meaning. The same is true with the amendment as written. Brevity in drafting should not diminish rights or lead to redundancy. In the actual and the two hypothetical cases, the framers added (or are imagined to have added) the same language—the same limitation on congressional power—and the only credible way to read that language is to recognize that the Press Clause guarantees freedoms to something called "the press" that the Speech Clause does not guarantee to everyone.

The argument that the Press Clause creates no distinct rights despite its presence in the text of the amendment is belied by the Supreme Court's many decisions recognizing a First Amendment right that, unlike the Press Clause, is *not* explicit in its text—freedom of association.[15] For we would then be saying that one freedom is not there even though it literally is, while another freedom is there even though it literally isn't. In the 1950s, Alabama state courts held the NAACP in contempt and fined it $100,000 after it refused to reveal the identities of its members from Alabama. In the Supreme Court, the association argued that the First

Amendment, through the Due Process Clause of the Fourteenth Amendment, protected its members' freedom of association. It argued that forcing disclosure of its members' identities violated that freedom. But there was one problem. The First Amendment does not mention freedom of association. That did not, however, trouble the Court, which reversed the contempt:

> Effective advocacy of both public and private points of view, particularly controversial ones, is undeniably enhanced by group association, as this Court has more than once recognized by remarking upon the close nexus between the freedoms of speech and assembly. It is beyond debate that freedom to engage in association for the advancement of beliefs and ideas is an inseparable aspect of the "liberty" assured by the Due Process Clause of the Fourteenth Amendment, which embraces freedom of speech. . . .
>
> Petitioner has made an uncontroverted showing that on past occasions revelation of the identity of its rank-and-file members has exposed these members to economic reprisal, loss of employment, threat of physical coercion, and other manifestations of public hostility. Under these circumstances, we think it apparent that compelled disclosure of petitioner's Alabama membership is likely to affect adversely the ability of petitioner and its members to pursue their collective effort to foster beliefs which they admittedly have the right to advocate, in that it may induce members to withdraw from the Association and dissuade others from joining it because of fear of exposure of their beliefs shown through their associations and of the consequences of this exposure.[16]

The Court's treatment of the First Amendment's Petition Clause also supports an independent existence for the Press Clause. The First Amendment says "Congress shall make no law . . . abridging . . . the right of the people . . . to petition the Government for a redress of grievances." A redundancy argument might also purge the Petition Clause. Petitions, like speech, are composed of words. The argument would assert that the Speech Clause protects all of the rights encompassed by the Petition Clause (and more), so the Petition Clause is redundant. Yet the Court has disagreed. While acknowledging some, perhaps substantial, overlap between the two clauses, the Court in 2001 recognized a separate dominion for the Petition Clause:

> Both speech and petition are integral to the democratic process, although not necessarily in the same way. The right to petition allows citizens to express their ideas, hopes, and concerns to their government and their elected representatives, whereas the right to speak fosters the public exchange of ideas that is integral to deliberative democracy as well as to the whole realm of ideas and human affairs. . . .
>
> Courts should not presume there is always an essential equivalence in the two Clauses or that Speech Clause precedents necessarily and in every case resolve Petition Clause claims. . . . Interpretation of the Petition Clause must be guided by the objectives and aspirations that underlie the right. A petition conveys the special concerns of its author to the government and, in its usual form, requests action by the government to address those concerns.[17]

The same should be true of the Press Clause.

If the answer to the first textual question is that the Press Clause is not redundant of the Speech Clause, one or both of the clauses must protect freedoms that the other does not. That leads to the second textual question. Do the two clauses protect different freedoms for different (if overlapping) populations? If so, some entity called "the press" is guaranteed protections that the Speech Clause denies others. Or do the two clauses protect different freedoms for the same population? If so, everyone who enjoys the freedoms guaranteed by the Speech Clause also enjoys the (somewhat) different freedoms guaranteed by the Press Clause, in which case there is no need to define the press—everyone would be the press.

The text gives us some clues. What should we make of the fact that the Speech Clause protects "the freedom of speech" whereas the Press Clause protects the "the freedom . . . of *the* press?" "Speech" and "press" are both nouns. But "freedom of speech" is synonymous with "freedom to speak." Speech implies speaking. What does "the press" imply? Perhaps the framers meant to distinguish the spoken word from the written word and assign different protections for each. But then why didn't they write "the freedom of speech and writing" or "the freedom to speak and to write?" And why would the framers have distinguished between spoken and written words in the first place? If they intended no distinction, they could have saved us a lot of trouble simply by prohibiting Congress from "abridging the freedom of expression" and have done with it.

Perhaps the framers feared that Congress would view written expression as capable of causing greater harm than speech and wanted explicitly to protect everyone's freedom to publish. But if that was the thinking, the framers could have protected against congressional abridgement of "the freedom of speech *or to publish.*" Instead, they wrote "or of the press," using the definite article, which strongly implies that the framers wanted to protect publishing by something or someone called the press, not by everyone.

Although the historical record has been cited for various interpretations of "the press," among them a claim that it refers solely to the printing press,[18] we can and should choose an interpretation that best enables the press to serve democracy in the United States, so long as our reading is not directly contradicted by credible contemporaneous evidence. With that as our purpose, we should read the Press Clause to refer to the press and not to all writing. We can and should read it to give "the press" rights that the Speech Clause does not give everyone. This reading avoids redundancy in two ways. It treats members of the press as a narrower category than all writers or speakers, and it protects the press in ways the Speech Clause does not protect all expression. But now we have made our task difficult for other reasons. Now we must answer two new questions: First, who or what is "the press" that the Press Clause protects? Second, what freedoms, beyond those already encompassed by the Speech Clause, does the Press Clause protect from abridgment?

The traditional method for lawyers and judges to answer questions like these is, once again, to review the historical record and try to discover precisely what the framers had in mind. Or at least to begin that way, although some would stop there. A different (or supplementary) method is to search for answers that are right for the nation today and consistent with the values and principles we discern behind the text. Answers to this inquiry will vary. But we don't ask it expecting consensus. We ask it to establish that we have the right to ask it, that the meaning of a constitutional term is not time bound. By doing so, we cross a threshold. We can go beyond the historical record and take up the question fresh as a matter of policy. A fair reading of Supreme Court opinions addressing press freedom in the past half-century tells us that this is exactly what the Court has done, sometimes explicitly. When the Court interprets broad constitutional principles, it is really making public policy, albeit dressed up with legal language and methodology.

THE PRESS CLAUSE IN
THE SUPREME COURT

If the Supreme Court had consistently rejected a separate role for the Press Clause in any circumstance, a contrary claim would be difficult. But it hasn't. The Court has often and emphatically recognized the importance of the Press Clause to American democracy. And then it no longer did so, without dealing forthrightly with the reversal or even recognizing its own contrary precedent. The Court's sleight of hand is apparent in its 2010 decision in *Citizens United v. Federal Election Commission*.[19] *Citizens United* is, of course, controversial for rejecting limits on corporate spending to influence federal elections. My focus is different. Largely overlooked is the Court's use of its opinion to reject any distinct role for the Press Clause.

The federal law in *Citizens United* prohibited corporations and unions from using their general treasury funds to influence elections for federal office through independent expenditures made within thirty or sixty days of a primary or general election. The law exempted "media corporations." In a 5–4 opinion, Justice Kennedy wrote that the law was unconstitutional as applied to nonmedia corporations. The Court ruled that corporations—Citizens United was a nonprofit corporation—had a First Amendment right to spend money to influence voters; the law's restrictions violated that right. The Court could have stopped right there because that was the sole question before it. "*Question*: Can Congress forbid the designated expenditures by nonmedia companies? *Answer*: No."

But Kennedy went much further. He used the law's exemption of media corporations to erase any constitutionally recognized role for the press.

> There is no precedent supporting laws that attempt to distinguish between corporations [that] are deemed to be exempt as media corporations and those [that] are not. "*We have consistently rejected the proposition that the institutional press has any constitutional privilege beyond that of other speakers.*" With the advent of the Internet and the decline of print and broadcast media, moreover, the line between the media and others who wish to comment on political and social issues becomes far more blurred.[20]

In this excerpt's quoted sentence, Kennedy reached out to nullify the Press Clause. But *Citizens United* was not about "any constitutional privilege" for the media. It was about the law's prohibition on nonmedia spending "expressly advocating the election or defeat of a candidate" for political office. Having said more than the case required, Kennedy then claimed that the Court had "consistently" rejected "any constitutional privilege" for the institutional press. That's not true. What it had done (though not "consistently") is reject the claim that lawmakers could impose limits on political spending by nonmedia companies (or otherwise limit their speech) in ways that lawmakers could not limit the spending of others.

Consider Kennedy's support for the sentence quoted in the excerpt above. Where does it come from? Kennedy cites a 1990 *dissent* by Justice Scalia.[21] Since it's a dissent, it means that the Scalia opinion did not command a majority of the Court. So how could Scalia, and therefore Kennedy, refer to what "we," meaning the Court, "have consistently rejected?" To support the plural pronoun, Scalia in turn relied on the Court's 1978 opinion in *First National Bank of Boston v. Bellotti*[22] and authorities it cited. But when we read *Bellotti*, we see that it actually *contradicts* Kennedy's and Scalia's broad claim of what the Court has "consistently" said. This is an omission that an editor would not tolerate from a reporter.

The issue in *Bellotti* was whether a Massachusetts criminal law could prevent a nonmedia corporation, a bank, from spending its own money to influence the outcome of a ballot measure. The state argued that the bank could not rely on the First Amendment because it was not "the press." The Court ruled for the bank:

> The press cases emphasize the special and constitutionally recognized role of that institution in informing and educating the public, offering criticism, and providing a forum for discussion and debate. But the press does not have a monopoly on either the First Amendment or the ability to enlighten.[23] Similarly, the Court's decisions involving corporations in the business of communication or entertainment are based not only on the role of the First Amendment in fostering individual self-expression

but also on its role in affording the public access to discussion, debate, and the dissemination of information and
ideas.[24]

Bellotti did *not* say that the press does not have "any constitutional privilege beyond that of other speakers," as Kennedy
wrote in *Citizens United*. Or that the Court has "consistently
rejected [that] proposition." It said only that the press did not
have a "monopoly" on the kind of speech that happened to be
at issue in *Bellotti* or, now, in *Citizens United*. It said nothing
about other ways—for example, by protection for newsgathering or of confidential sources—in which the Press Clause
may protect the work of the press. Equally troubling, although
Kennedy cited *Bellotti* many times, he ignored the first sentence in the excerpt above. That sentence says the exact
opposite of what Kennedy claimed in *Citizens United*. It
acknowledges "the special and constitutionally recognized
role" of the press. *Bellotti*, in turn, supported the sentence that
Kennedy ignored with a citation to the Court's opinion in
Mills v. Alabama,[25] which embraced the Press Clause (and
which I discuss presently). *Mills* and other cases contradict
Kennedy's sweeping statement in *Citizens United*. Yet Kennedy
ignored them, too. Further unpacking the errors in Kennedy's
effort to neuter the Press Clause is best left to a note.[26]

In decades past, the Court has endorsed a distinct role for
the Press Clause. In 1966, Justice Black, writing for a majority
of eight justices in *Mills v. Alabama*,[27] invalidated a law that
made "it a crime for the editor of a daily newspaper to write
and publish an editorial on election day urging people to vote
a certain way on issues submitted to them." Black wrote:

The Constitution specifically selected the press, which
includes not only newspapers, books, and magazines, but

also humble leaflets and circulars [citing *Lovell v. City of Griffin* (1938), discussed below], to play an important role in the discussion of public affairs. Thus the press serves and was designed to serve as a powerful antidote to any abuses of power by governmental officials and as a constitutionally chosen means for keeping officials elected by the people responsible to all the people whom they were selected to serve. Suppression of the right of the press to praise or criticize governmental agents and to clamor and contend for or against change, which is all that this editorial did, muzzles one of the very agencies the Framers of our Constitution thoughtfully and deliberately selected to improve our society and keep it free.[28]

Mills v. Alabama's embrace of the Press Clause is even more emphatic because of its citation to *Lovell v. City of Griffin*. *Lovell* presented a challenge to a local ordinance that made it a "nuisance" to "distribut[e], either by hand or otherwise, circulars, handbooks, advertising, or literature of any kind" without a permit from the city manager.[29] Alma Lovell had handed out "a pamphlet and magazine in the nature of religious tracts, setting forth the gospel of the 'Kingdom of Jehovah.'" She did not have a permit and was convicted of violating the ordinance and sentenced to fifty days in jail because she did not or could not pay the $50 fine.[30] The unanimous Court said the ordinance "strikes at the very foundation of the freedom of the press."[31] In finding it unconstitutional, the *Lovell* Court relied on the Press Clause and this definition of the press:

The liberty of the press is not confined to newspapers and periodicals. It necessarily embraces pamphlets and leaflets. These indeed have been historic weapons in the defense of liberty, as the pamphlets of Thomas Paine and others in our own history abundantly attest. The press in its historic connotation comprehends every sort of publication which affords a vehicle of information and opinion.[32]

Mills could have relied solely on the Speech Clause, but it looked to the Press Clause instead. "The question," Black wrote, "is whether it abridges freedom of the press for a State to punish a newspaper editor for doing no more than publishing an editorial on election day urging people to vote a particular way in the election."[33]

Mills's focus on the function of the press (what it does, not how it is organized) also appears in *Cox Broadcasting Corp. v. Cohn*,[34] another decision that today's Court prefers to overlook. A television station was sued for invasion of privacy when, in violation of state law, it identified a rape victim whose name it had lawfully obtained from court records. In 1975, the Court ruled for the station. In his opinion for the Court, Justice White wrote: "In this sphere of collision between claims of privacy and those of the free press, the interests on both sides are plainly rooted in the traditions and significant concerns of our society."[35] He then proceeded to single out the special position of the press in a way that perfectly describes its watchdog role.

In the first place, in a society in which each individual has but limited time and resources with which to observe at first hand the operations of his government, he relies necessarily upon the press to bring to him in convenient form the facts of those operations. Great responsibility is accordingly placed upon the news media to report fully and accurately the proceedings of government, and official records and documents open to the public are the basic data of governmental operations. Without the information provided by the press most of us and many of our representatives would be unable to vote intelligently or to register opinions on the administration of government generally. With respect to judicial proceedings in particular, the function of the press serves to guarantee the fairness of trials and to bring to bear the beneficial effects of public scrutiny upon the administration of justice.[36]

This language is a powerful validation of the centrality of the press to democracy, which *Citizens United* made no effort to refute. It chose instead to ignore it. *Cox Broadcasting* is cited with twenty-two other cases solely for the proposition that corporations enjoy First Amendment rights.[37]

Even *Branzburg v. Hayes*,[38] the famously controversial 1972 case that rejected the claim that a "newsman" had a privilege to refuse to reveal confidential sources when subpoenaed by a grand jury, acknowledged, if begrudgingly, that the Press Clause did give the press some, if vague, protection for newsgathering, a quintessential press activity. Justice White wrote: "We do not question the significance of free speech, press, or assembly to the country's welfare. Nor is it suggested that newsgathering does not qualify for First Amendment protection; without some protection for seeking out the news, freedom of the press could be eviscerated."[39]

The Court's respect for the Press Clause waned nearly to the vanishing point between its 1966 decision in *Mills* and its 2010 decision in *Citizens United*. And "nearly" may be optimistic. What explains this? One answer may be that the justices, like First Amendment scholars, realize that history will be of little help in deciding the meaning of the clause. Framer intent is elusive, as the Court recognized in 1983 when it overturned a Minnesota tax on a publications use of paper and ink. Relying on work of the prominent First Amendment scholar Zechariah Chafee, Justice O'Connor wrote:

> It is true that our opinions rarely speculate on precisely how the Framers would have analyzed a given regulation of expression. In general, though, we have only limited evidence of exactly how the Framers intended the First Amendment to apply. There are no recorded debates in the Senate or in the States, and the discussion in the House of Representatives was couched in general terms, perhaps in response to Madison's suggestion that the Representatives not stray from simple acknowledged principles. . . . Consequently, we ordinarily simply apply those general principles, requiring the government to justify any burdens on First Amendment rights by showing that they are necessary to achieve a legitimate overriding governmental interest.[40]

The Court treated the tax challenge under the Press Clause, not the Speech Clause. How could it credibly do otherwise? The plaintiff was a newspaper, and the law taxed paper and ink. Only the Press Clause made sense.

Opaque constitutional history cannot alone explain the Court's disregard of the Press Clause. As the Court wrote in the Minnesota tax case, when it doesn't know the framers' mind, it construes the "general principles" embedded in their language. So a second reason why the Court is turning away from the Press Clause may be out of concern for the practical problems it believed would follow. In *Branzburg*, Justice White said as much:

The administration of a constitutional newsman's privilege would present practical and conceptual difficulties of a high order. Sooner or later, it would be necessary to define those categories of newsmen who qualified for the privilege, a questionable procedure in light of the traditional doctrine that liberty of the press is the right of the lonely pamphleteer who uses carbon paper or a mimeograph just as much as of the large metropolitan publisher who utilizes the latest photocomposition methods.[41]

The definitional question is indeed a challenge but hardly insurmountable. As we shall see in chapter 2, it has not stopped the Court from construing the word "religion" in the First Amendment's Free Exercise Clause, a task at least as daunting. Nor has it stopped lower courts and lawmakers, including Congress, from defining the press, including on the very issue presented in *Branzburg*—the right not to reveal the identity of a confidential source. The fact that framer intent is elusive should encourage us to focus on the proper role (and responsibility) of the press in America today and how best to protect it. We can ask what, as a matter of policy, the Press Clause should be held to say. We have a precedent for such bold rethinking from the Supreme Court, which dramatically expanded constitutional protection for expression in the last four decades of the twentieth century. Revolution is not an exaggeration for what the Court did. Beginning in 1964, with *New York Times v. Sullivan*,[42] and in opinions that built on *New York Times* in the ensuing decades, the Court has interpreted the First Amendment to protect the press and others in ways that cannot be traced, even dimly, to the framers' intent in 1789, when the First Amendment was proposed. The Court adapted the "general principles" behind the

amendment to the needs of the nation in the twentieth century.[43] It created an intricate set of doctrines to enable the
press to do the job American democracy needed. The *New
York Times* decision and decisions that build on it are a powerful rebuttal to the Court's present timidity in developing a
jurisprudence for the Press Clause.

THE ERA OF *NEW YORK TIMES V. SULLIVAN*

A Montgomery, Alabama, city commissioner, who was
responsible for public safety, sued the *New York Times* and
four African American clergymen. He alleged that a full-
page advertisement that the clergymen had placed in the
paper libeled him. The advertisement criticized as excessive
the police response to a black student protest on the Alabama
State College campus. Some minor facts were false. A false
fact is not a libel unless it harms someone's reputation. The
state court jury thought that the false facts in the *Times*
advertisement did harm the commissioner's reputation and
awarded him $500,000. The Supreme Court reversed.[44] It
ruled that the Constitution required that a public official
like the commissioner prove that the defendants acted with
"actual malice," which it defined to mean that the allegedly
libelous statement was made "with knowledge that it was
false or with reckless disregard of whether it was false or not."
"Reckless disregard" is not, as often assumed, an extreme
version of ordinary negligence. It does not mean "careless" or
"sloppy." "Reckless disregard" means that although a libel
defendant may not have *known* that a statement was false, he
just didn't care whether it was false or not. Actual malice is a

subjective test. It asks what the defendant actually knew or believed. It does not matter that another journalist, perhaps a more careful journalist, would have acted differently.[45]

In the *New York Times* case, the Court also said a public official who brings a defamation claim must prove "actual malice" with "convincing clarity." A plaintiff's burden of proof in most civil cases is lower. It is a preponderance of the evidence, which can be described as meaning "more likely than not." A 51–49 level of confidence satisfies this lower burden of proof. "Convincing clarity," which is also described as "clear and convincing evidence," is more demanding, although not susceptible to an arithmetic formula. The Court went on to hold that the commissioner's evidence did not prove actual malice with convincing clarity.

The *New York Times* case can easily be read as a Press Clause case. After all, the lead defendant was a newspaper, and the Court's opinion did emphasize the importance of a free press in American history. But if the case had been decided on the basis of the Press Clause alone, the clergymen who placed the advertisement would have lost because they were certainly not the press. Instead, they successfully relied on the First Amendment's Speech Clause. The Court cited both the Speech Clause and the Press Clause of the First Amendment, but throughout it emphasized the origin of the Press Clause.

The day *New York Times* came down can rightly be seen as the first day of the modern American era of press freedom. The ruling upended a century and a half of conventional wisdom. In the years following, the Court applied *New York Times* to persons who were "public figures" but not public officials—that is, persons who held no public office but whose fame or power justified giving the press added constitutional protection against libel claims.[46] The public has as legitimate an interest in news about them as it does in news about public officials. The Court later ruled that public officials and public figures (collectively, public persons) who sue a media defendant must prove that an allegedly libelous statement was in fact false. Traditionally, a libel defendant has had the burden of proving that what he said about the plaintiff was true. Truth is a complete defense to a libel claim. But when the plaintiff is a public person, the burden shifts. The plaintiff must prove that an allegedly libelous statement was false.[47]

There's more. In the decades following the 1964 *New York Times* decision, the Court erected First Amendment defenses to actions for damages when the claim was *not* based on libel but on some other theory. In each of these cases, the press was the most prominent and often the only defendant. Indeed, none of the cases would likely have been brought but for the fact of publication or broadcast. In one case, in violation of a state statute, a newspaper had reported the name of a rape victim, which it had learned from public reports. Because the report was true, the victim could not sue for libel. She instead sued for invasion of privacy. The Court said the First Amendment protected the publication. Although it did not say which clause in the amendment applied, the opinion repeatedly cited the interests of "the press" in being able to publish true information.[48] In a second case, Jerry Falwell won a judgment against *Hustler* for emotional damages after it published a mock Campari-like advertisement implying that Falwell's "first time" had been with his mother. Citing the First Amendment, the Court reversed.[49]

And then, in *Bartnicki v. Vopper,*[50] an opinion whose full significance cannot yet be known, the Court confronted a damages claim against a radio station. In violation of a federal statute, the station had broadcast a recording of a telephone conversation that an unidentified third person had illegally intercepted. That person put the recording in the mailbox of a man named Yocum, who gave it to the station. The broadcast conversation, between officers of a teachers' union, could be understood to threaten violence during a labor dispute. The officers sued the station, relying on its violation of the federal statute. The Court rejected their claim. It cited the First Amendment and, among other precedents, the Pentagon Papers case, which the Court characterized as upholding "the right of the press to publish information of great public concern obtained from documents stolen by a third party."[51] The proposition that the public's interest in learning about the threats could insulate the station (and Yocum) from liability for the broadcast—a liability that a federal statute expressly created—has profound consequences (explored in chapter 5) whenever the source for a press story is an illegal or unauthorized leak.

Even in years when the Court appeared to dismiss the Press Clause as redundant, it has twice recognized the possibility of a preferred position for "media defendants." In *Philadelphia Newspapers v. Hepps* (1986), the Court ruled that a private person (i.e., not a public official or public figure) who "seeks damages against a media defendant for speech of public concern" must prove that an alleged defamatory statement was false.[52] It pointedly declined to say if the same burden would apply if the defendant were a "nonmedia defendant."[53] The Court reiterated the media-versus-nonmedia distinction four years later in *Milkovich v. Lorain Journal, Co.*, which held that opinions can be the basis for defamation claims if they imply false facts.[54] Justice Kennedy ignored both of these cases in *Citizens United*, when he wrote (quoting a dissent of Justice Scalia) that "we have consistently rejected the proposition that the institutional press has any constitutional privilege beyond that of other speakers."[55] *Hepps* and *Milkovich* did not reject that proposition.[56] Kennedy did cite *Hepps*, but only for the uncontroversial proposition that corporations enjoy First Amendment rights.[57]

The cases beginning with *New York Times* are significant not only because of the particular First Amendment protections they fashioned but also because the Court recognized the new constitutional protections in the first place. These cases upended First Amendment law from what it had been for nearly two centuries. Although the opinion in *New York Times* cited many authorities and speeches at the time of the founding and later, all describing the importance of freedom of speech and freedom of the press, none of the authorities implied or anticipated the elaborate constitutional edifice that the Court erected in 1964 and ensuing decades to impede defamation and other claims based on a publication. And although the Court cited both the Speech and Press Clauses in these opinions and sometimes held that their protection extended to nonpress defendants as well, in many of the important cases the sole defendant was a member of the press.

What the Court has done, then, is create, out of nearly nothing—out of nine highly elastic words ("abridging the freedom of speech, or of the press") and an enlightened appreciation for the importance of a free press—nearly impregnable constitutional defenses to state or federal claims if the plaintiff is a public person, if the subject is a matter of public concern, or if the information is true and lawfully received, even if the source is violating a duty to others or has obtained the information illegally. Beginning in 1964, in short, the Court rewrote the meaning of the Speech and Press Clauses. "The truth," Burt Neuborne has written, "is that the First Amendment as we know it today didn't exist before Justice William Brennan Jr. and the rest of the Warren Court invented it in the 1960s."[58] With this precedent so starkly deviating from earlier views, there should be no need to apologize for proposals that advocate continuation of the evolution the Court has undertaken in order best to serve the nation in the twenty-first century.

THE PRESS CLAUSE AND INVESTIGATIVE REPORTING

We cannot begin to describe how the Press Clause or legislation should protect freedom of the press in American life without asking why protection is needed—that is, protection beyond what the Speech Clause or other constitutional provisions give everyone. Why does democracy need the press? The question of need (usually framed as about role) has been asked and answered so often that it may seem unnecessary to address it. Yet in the context of the arguments in this book, it is a bedrock question. The two critical words are "protect" and "need." The scope of the protection must respond to the nature of the need.

What is the need? Thomas Emerson's 1970 book *The System of Freedom of Expression* contains a sweeping and influential explanation of the purposes of the First Amendment. Emerson, a Yale law professor, offered four "premises" or justifications for the amendment. Freedom of expression, he wrote, (1) "is essential as a means of assuring individual self-fulfillment," (2) "is an essential process for advancing knowledge and discovering truth," (3) "is essential to provide for participation in decision making by all members of society," and (4) "is a method of achieving a more adaptable and hence a more stable community."[59] Emerson was defending freedom of all expression. The Press Clause serves all four premises but most clearly serves the second and third.

We can begin with subtraction. Most of what the press publishes today will not encounter government interference or lead to legal liability. The Supreme Court's decisions in the *New York Times* line of cases should protect all but the most oblivious (or malicious) journalist and editor from liability for publication of stories they deem newsworthy. Included in this safe zone are coverage of executive and legislative proceedings or actions, much local and foreign news, consumer news, political news, food recipes, home-decorating advice, medical discoveries, press-conference coverage, science coverage, court decisions, wedding announcements, crime reports, traffic accidents, the weather, obituaries, cultural coverage and reviews, travel advice, sports news, society news, the real-estate market, and financial news. Look at a daily newspaper and subtract these stories. Not much remains.

I recognize the importance of these stories. We make decisions based on them and would miss them if they were gone. Many stories do something else too, something easily overlooked and, although incidental to my argument, quite important. They create a shared experience of the world we live in—the larger world and our local world. We might even say that by providing a common experience, the stories (and the editors who assign them and the reporters who find them) contribute to a sense of community (Emerson's fourth premise) because many people will read and may then discuss the same stories.

Among the stories remaining after subtracting those that should not confront legal (as opposed to financial) impediments are investigative stories and stories based on confidential sources, distinct but overlapping categories. These stories serve as an antagonist to powerful private and public institutions and public persons by disclosing information they may prefer to conceal but that an author or editor has judged important for the public to know. With the defenses afforded by the *New York Times* line of cases and a little care, liability based on the content of investigative stories should ordinarily be avoidable.

Even if a journalist's source violates a legal duty, the press should remain free to publish what it lawfully receives. The Court has never said as much, but it has come close. For example, in *Landmark Communications, Inc. v. Virginia*, a newspaper reported that a judge was under investigation by a judicial-conduct commission, whose work was confidential under state law. The paper's unidentified source may have violated Virginia law by disclosing the investigation to the newspaper. The state prosecuted and convicted the newspaper for publishing an unauthorized leak. In the Supreme Court, the newspaper urged "as the dispositive answer to the question presented that truthful reporting about public officials in connection with their public duties is always insulated from the imposition of criminal sanctions by the First Amendment." The Court would not go so far as to say "always." It reversed the conviction on narrower grounds:

> We find it unnecessary to adopt this categorical approach to resolve the issue before us. We conclude that the publication Virginia seeks to punish under its statute lies near

the core of the First Amendment, and the Commonwealth's interests advanced by the imposition of criminal sanctions are insufficient to justify the actual and potential encroachments on freedom of speech and of the press which follow therefrom.[60]

The Court has continued to find it "unnecessary to adopt [the] categorical approach." Consequently, it remains possible, though highly unlikely, that on the right facts the press can be sued or prosecuted for publishing lawfully received truthful information that editors deem newsworthy.[61]

CHALLENGES TO INVESTIGATIVE REPORTING BEYOND THE LAW

Although the law today should rarely pose a threat to the *content* of investigative stories, it may pose obstacles to getting the story in the first place. Those obstacles are to newsgathering and the ability to protect the identity of confidential sources, subjects addressed in chapters 4 and 5. Beyond the law, however, other obstacles are cost, public apathy, and lately the specter of wealthy persons bringing or funding claims against the press despite the unlikelihood of winning. A partial remedy for this last danger is a strong anti-SLAPP law, a subject of chapter 6.

Of public apathy, little can be said with confidence. Measuring the level of engagement is nearly impossible for stories in print. Measurement is easier online. Clicks and time online can be counted, but investigative stories tend to be lengthy, and competition for attention is keen. Reading a two-thousand-word story while going to or from work, or in a weekly or monthly magazine (where the story may be longer), requires a commitment of time. Sources of entertainment online and the hundreds of channels that populate cable television compete for the same time. Unless a story's revelation is astonishing, will people care enough to read to the end or even to start reading?

Apathy has always been a challenge. Only 58 percent of those eligible voted in the presidential election of 2016.[62] In 2014, an off year, 36.4 percent of those eligible voted.[63] Of course, a correspondence between apathy about voting and apathy about the news will not be exact. Americans may closely follow the news about a presidential, mayoral, or congressional election yet fail to vote. Or more may vote than bother to learn much about the candidates or the issues. Nonetheless, the degree of voter apathy, even for president, surely tells us something dispiriting about public engagement, including engagement with the news. A 2010 Pew Research Center Study found that Americans spend seventy minutes a day learning the news. Nearly half that time—thirty-two minutes—was spent watching television news, and ten minutes were spent with print newspapers. Respondents under thirty spent a total of forty-five minutes on the news each day.[64]

While apathy may lead to disengagement from news, cloistering, as I'll call it, restricts the news that is encountered. Time and attention being finite, a multiplicity of electronic and print sources can erode shared experience by enabling members of the public to choose to see, listen to, or read only within a narrow spectrum of information that interests them, thereby shrinking the opportunity for chance and surprise and the extent to which others will see or hear the same stories. Of course, news consumers have always been selective.

No one reads everything in a magazine or newspaper. But in turning pages, one might happen upon stories they would not have thought to look for. Serendipity suffers in a highly fragmented market where algorithms (or hidden curators) give each of us the stories we have (or it has) decided we want and those only. The discrepancies are aggravated when ideological positions cause consumers to block or ignore sources that challenge their preferences. "When it comes to getting news about politics and government, liberals and conservatives inhabit different worlds. There is little overlap in the news sources they turn to and trust. And whether discussing politics online or with friends, they are more likely than others to interact with like-minded individuals," Pew reported in 2014.[65] After the 2016 election, a Pew survey found that "Americans who say they voted for Trump in the general election relied heavily on Fox News as their main source of election news leading up to the 2016 election, whereas Clinton voters named an array of different sources, with no one source named by more than one-in-five of her supporters."[66]

Beyond apathy, we must also address cost. Investigative stories require much time and money. A publication must be able to defend the expense unless charitable or ideological motives inspire its owners, or, for nonprofit organizations, its donors, to absorb the cost. How to support this work as advertising dollars decline and if an uninterested or distracted public is unwilling to pay for it is a challenge the internet has exacerbated through its effect on circulation and advertising. Pew reports that total ad revenue for newspapers (digital and print combined) fell from $43.4 billion in 2007 to an estimated $18.3 billion in 2016, itself down from an estimated $20.4 billion in 2015. In the decade 2007–2016, circulation revenue increased slightly from $10.2 billion in 2007 to an estimated $10.9 billion in 2016.[67]

When the money was there, publications could fund investigations even if few readers paid serious attention. The advertisers paid for the work, consumers paid the advertisers (by buying), and a newspaper could use the advertising money for investigative reporting. While the newspaper would hope that its stories resonated broadly, as often they did, it may not have mattered if they did not, so long as editors deemed that a story addressed a matter of public concern, influential members of the public read it, and the advertising money continued. For their part, the advertisers may have had little or no interest in the stories their money made possible (or may even have disliked them). Circulation justified the cost of the advertising. In this way, supply did not have to correlate with demand.

This triangular relationship (advertisers, readers, newspapers) served the respective interests well enough for most of the twentieth century. But decline in advertising dollars has forced the questions: Will readers pay to make up for the loss of advertising revenue? Will others? If the press is necessary to our system of government, should the public, through public funding, support media investigations, just as it is obligated to support the three branches of government? And how might that be done while ensuring independence? Public money for investigative journalism is a subject of chapter 6.

WE ARE *NOT* ALL JOURNALISTS NOW

With freedom to imagine the proper role of the press in the American political and constitutional order, urging the law to catch up, we can return to some fundamental questions that it will be necessary to answer in the following chapters.

Who or what is "the press" of the Press Clause? In a constitutional structure that relies on federalism and separation of powers to prevent the concentration of unchecked power in one branch of government, or worse, among a small number of people, what or who will check abuse of power by the press? Or to put it another way, what will we require from those who want to enjoy the extra freedoms that the Press Clause grants beyond the Speech Clause? The press does not get unchecked power. No one does. Who will decide who may enjoy those freedoms and whether they have been abused? For much of our history, threats of defamation lawsuits or liability for privacy invasion or for certain newsgathering methods did the work of checking against press abuses, although not always fairly. Court rulings have much reduced, although they have not eliminated, the threat of successful litigation. What then remains as a check against abuse by the press? This last question presents a particular challenge. It would be unworkable to let government officials decide if the press has complied with the requirements that entitle it to the protections of the Press Clause. They or their colleagues and supporters may be the target of news stories. But then who will decide?

Answers to these and other questions occupy much of this book, but I partly preview my answer to the question "who or what is the press?" by saying what it is not. I reject the claim that we are all journalists now.[68] This claim posits that because technology enables anyone to write about anything and distribute what they write to everyone, everyone is (or can be) a journalist and apparently entitled to all of the same Press Clause protections as everybody else. I recognize the good intentions of those who claim that everyone can, today, be a journalist. Nonetheless, the idea is dangerous. It trivializes the press and press ethics and will weaken or eliminate a distinct role for the Press Clause.

Press ethics (discussed in chapter 3) is what makes journalism a profession. But whether or not journalists accept the label "profession" to describe their work, it is press ethics that justifies the freedoms the Press Clause should be understood to guarantee and that legislation should expand. Without the restraints that ethics rules (or call them journalistic standards) place on how the press exercises its powers, courts and lawmakers will be inclined to describe press freedoms narrowly or no broader than the Speech Clause. That in turn will impede journalists and press organizations whose work (on behalf of society) would otherwise benefit from a broad definition of press freedom, whether grounded in the Press Clause, legislation, or court decisions. Echoing the themes in this chapter, Sonja West has identified the problem.

> A broad definition of the press, somewhat ironically, results in fewer press rights overall. For the Press Clause to mean something independent of the Speech Clause, it necessarily cannot apply to everyone. If every individual is also a journalist or every message is also news, then there is no need for two distinct clauses. . . . The justices' understandable desire to avoid favoring an elite group has led them to allow the Speech Clause to swallow up the Press Clause. In other words, the otherwise admirable and democratic objective to leave no one out of the press club creates a boomerang effect that results in no club at all.[69]

I accept that many people who would not qualify as journalists publish much information that will enrich society, and I agree that their work should be vigorously protected, which can be done via the Speech Clause, legislation, and court decisions. But the added protections of the Press Clause should belong to journalists only. My next task is to define "the press" and describe the added protections.

2

WHAT AND WHO IS "THE PRESS"?

I f the Press Clause is an autonomous source of rights, whatever those rights may be, we must next identify the press. Who or what is the press? In *Branzburg v. Hayes* (1972),[1] Justice White cited the difficulty in defining the press as one reason to reject a constitutional "newsman's privilege" to refuse to disclose the identity of a source in response to a grand jury subpoena. Before we get to that, however, a short detour to a different First Amendment question may enlighten. What is religion? Recall that the First Amendment says that Congress (and by extension the states) "shall make no law respecting an establishment of religion, or prohibiting the free exercise thereof." The first clause is the Establishment Clause. The government cannot designate an official religion or favor one religion over others. The second clause is the Free Exercise Clause. Free-exercise claims arise when a law imposes obligations that are well within the state's power, but a person claims that the requirement violates his religion. Which of the two will give way? The person making the claim cannot be the sole arbiter of the question. Otherwise, avoidance of laws would be easy. So the courts must first say whether the asserted religion is a "religion" within the contemplation of the First Amendment and, if so, whether the law impedes its free exercise. If it does, they must then balance the state's interest in enforcing the law against the religious objections to compliance. Neither side always wins.

Wisconsin v. Yoder,[2] decided shortly before *Branzburg* rejected a "newsman's privilege," is an ideal case to see the Supreme Court's approach to the Free Exercise Clause. A valid Wisconsin law required parents to send their children to school until age sixteen. Two Amish parents were prosecuted when, for religious reasons, they refused to send their children to school beyond eighth grade. The Court recognized that merely citing a religious belief to avoid an otherwise valid state law would not do. The religion had to be a real religion.

> Although a determination of what is a "religious" belief or practice entitled to constitutional protection may present a most delicate question, the very concept of ordered liberty precludes allowing every person to make his own standards on matters of conduct in which society as a whole has important interests. Thus, if the Amish asserted their claims because of their subjective evaluation and rejection of the contemporary secular values accepted by the majority, much as Thoreau rejected the social values of his time and isolated himself at Walden Pond, their claims would not rest on a religious basis.[3]

But the Amish, the Court said, were not Thoreau. Their beliefs were religious, constitutionally speaking, even though Thoreau's were not. The Court wrote:

Aided by a history of three centuries as an identifiable
religious sect and a long history as a successful and self-
sufficient segment of American society, the Amish in this
case have convincingly demonstrated the sincerity of their
religious beliefs, the interrelationship of belief with their
mode of life, the vital role that belief and daily conduct
play in the continued survival of Old Order Amish com-
munities and their religious organization, and the hazards
presented by the State's enforcement of a statute generally
valid to others.[4]

We might think that "religion" would be as hard or harder
to define than "the press," but six weeks after *Yoder*, *Branzburg* balked at defining the press. In *Yoder*, of course, the
Court could not escape the task unless it was prepared to say
either that the Free Exercise Clause gave the Amish (and
therefore everyone else) no rights at all or that religion is
whatever anyone says it is. It was not about to say either of
these things. Yet it was quite willing in *Branzburg* and later
cases to say that the Press Clause gave the press (almost) no
rights at all because the Court could not define "the press."

Paradoxically, in the very act of explaining the difficulty in
defining the press, Justice White's *Branzburg* opinion (quoted
in chap. 1) then partly overcame it, but it did so by greatly
exaggerating the challenge the Court faced.

Liberty of the press is the right of the lonely pamphleteer
who uses carbon paper or a mimeograph just as much as of
the large metropolitan publisher who utilizes the latest
photocomposition methods. Freedom of the press is a
"fundamental personal right" which "is not confined to

newspapers and periodicals. It necessarily embraces pamphlets and leaflets. . . . The press in its historic connotation comprehends every sort of publication which affords a vehicle of information and opinion." The informative function asserted by representatives of the organized press in the present cases is also performed by lecturers, political pollsters, novelists, academic researchers, and dramatists. Almost any author may quite accurately assert that he is contributing to the flow of information to the public, that he relies on confidential sources of information, and that these sources will be silenced if he is forced to make disclosures before a grand jury.[5]

White is saying that in defining the press the Court could not limit the definition to the institutional press—to press organizations—but would have to include a host of others, including "the lonely pamphleteer," who convey information to the public. This is because press freedom "is a 'fundamental personal right,'" that is, not an institutional right. Fine. But why did a definition encompassing more than just the institutional press so trouble the Court? We see in White's list the foundation for an inclusive definition, one that focuses on function or task, not organizational or institutional affiliation. What one does, not where one does it, would become the test for membership.

This was not, of course, White's purpose. He meant to show that a definition was impractical if not impossible even as he began to develop one. We should ask instead whether the similarities between "newsmen" and some others on White's list would justify treating the others—the academic researcher, say—in the same way if they satisfied all conditions for inclusion in the category "the press." Or if "the

lonely pamphleteer"—Tom Paine comes to mind—is doing the
same work as the "newsman" affiliated with the institutional
press, we could just as well include Tom in the protection of
the Press Clause. Today, of course, Tom might be a blogger
or publish on social media. Yet it is that very prospect that
may explain the Court's continuing refusal to reexamine
Branzburg. Nearly anyone can be a twenty-first-century Tom
Paine. If nearly anyone who distributes information on any
platform can be the press, then the Press Clause would do no
distinct work. To avoid that, the universe of those who qualify for membership in the press must be appreciably smaller
than nearly anyone, and the Court would have to develop
criteria for shrinking it, which it has not done, though others
have.

White's list includes persons who are not within any conventional definition of the press, even a broad one. He identifies "dramatists" and "novelists." And then, just to show how
amorphous the category would truly be, he adds for good
measure "almost any author [who can] accurately assert that
he is contributing to the flow of information to the public."
The "almost any" argument did not stop the Court from
evaluating the religious claims of the Amish. "Almost any"
person may likewise claim that disobedience of a law—even
the very same law—is dictated by her "religion," but the
Court was nonetheless willing to evaluate that claim in *Yoder*
when asserted by the Amish. Why couldn't it do the same for
claims to be part of "the press?"

White makes a common legal argument, one that judges
are disinclined to accept when lawyers make them but that
judges themselves make when convenient: debunk the opposing position by proclaiming that it has no sensible limit and
can lead to absurd results, even if the result of accepting the

argument in the immediate circumstance would not be absurd. White does this when he includes novelists and dramatists on his list simply because they, like "newsmen," provide information to the public. Although providing information to the public is a necessary condition for press status, it is not alone sufficient. *The Iceman Cometh* and *The Red Badge of Courage* are not journalism, even though, in their fashion, they provide information to the public. True, we can imagine a play or novel that relies on original reporting secured with a confidentiality pledge that is later challenged in court. But White offers no such example. Listing dramatists and novelists must be seen as a rhetorical device meant to trivialize the journalists' claim. Pamphleteers, bloggers, and scholars, on the other hand, may be the press. Whether they are will depend on a richer definition of the press than the single, broad criterion White uses to build his case against defining the press.

White is correct, of course, that without a definition of the press, we cannot have a Press Clause, but fashioning a definition has not proved the challenge White predicted. The press has been defined multiple times outside the Supreme Court, including

- in state shield laws—laws that shield journalists from a finding of contempt if they refuse to disclose confidential (and sometimes, but less often, nonconfidential) sources;
- in the long-proposed but never adopted federal Free Flow of Information Act;
- in the federal Freedom of Information Act. Because the press gets a discount on the cost of providing documents it requests, it must be defined;

- in determining eligibility for press passes; and
- in lower federal court decisions.

A majority of the federal appellate courts (courts just below the Supreme Court) that have addressed the issue have read *Branzburg*, including a stray sentence in White's opinion—"Nor is it suggested that news gathering does not qualify for First Amendment protection; without some protection for seeking out the news, freedom of the press could be eviscerated"—to recognize a journalist's privilege in some circumstances. These courts have upheld a *qualified* reporter's privilege to protect a confidential, and even a nonconfidential, source when the demand for the information does not come from a grand jury, as it did in *Branzburg*. The privilege is called "qualified" because it is not absolute, which means that it can be overcome if the need is great, such as to prevent a terrorist act or find a kidnapped child. The decisions that recognize a qualified privilege are not identical in their definition of the press or the scope of the protection they afford. They are, however, largely consistent in grounding the privilege in the Press Clause of the First Amendment or in the entire amendment. Some lower court opinions are positively expansive (for courts) in describing the importance of the press and even the importance of investigative reporting. A minority of federal appellate courts disagrees. They say that the other courts are reading *Branzburg* to say the exact opposite of what the Supreme Court decided and that there is, therefore, no need to define the press.

Of immediate importance is not which definition of the press is correct but the fact that multiple sources, including other courts, have been able credibly to undertake the definitional task that spooked White, whether to protect the identity of a source, for the mundane job of issuing press passes, or in state laws that limit subpoenas to journalists. *Branzburg* left a blank space that other government actors have managed to fill. They did what *Branzburg* would not.

So to the task at hand: A living Press Clause needs a definition of the press. What shall it be? Four opinions from three federal appellate courts tell us. Especially influential has been the Second Circuit Court of Appeals, based in New York. It has not only managed to get around *Branzburg*; it has found in its language the exact opposite of what Justice White seems to have intended—a broad privilege for, and a definition of, the press.

Von Bulow v. von Bulow (1987)[6] was a civil lawsuit by Martha von Bulow (brought by her children on her behalf) against her husband Claus von Bulow, who was not the children's father and who had been prosecuted for and acquitted of assault with intent to kill Martha, in an incident that left her in a permanent coma. The subsequent civil lawsuit made a similar allegation against Claus. The legal issues in the civil case are irrelevant for our purposes, but what is relevant is the circuit court's ruling when Martha's children sought to subpoena documents from Andrea Reynolds, a friend of Claus. "Those documents consisted of investigative reports commissioned by Reynolds on the life-style of Martha von Bulow's children, notes taken by Reynolds while observing the criminal trial of von Bulow, and the manuscript to date of an unpublished book being written by Reynolds about the events surrounding the von Bulow prosecution."[7] Reynolds refused to produce the manuscript of the unpublished book, unsuccessfully cited the journalist's privilege, was held in contempt, and appealed. She relied in part on *Branzburg*. Because one reading of *Branzburg* is that there is no such thing as journalist's privilege, the Second Circuit might have rejected Reynolds's appeal summarily. But it did not.

> [In *Branzburg*], the Supreme Court held that a journalist does not have an absolute privilege under the First Amendment to refuse to appear and testify before a grand jury. . . . The Court rejected the claim of privilege, basing its decision on the traditional importance of grand juries and the strong public interest in effective criminal investigation. The Court recognized, however, that a qualified privilege may be proper in some circumstances because *newsgathering* was not without First Amendment protection.[8]

The conclusion in the final sentence would likely have astonished Justice White. Nonetheless, the Second Circuit then identified "certain principles" for evaluating a journalist's privilege claim. This is the challenge that so vexed White.

> [First, the qualified privilege] emanates from the strong public policy supporting the unfettered communication of information by the journalist to the public. Second, whether a person is a journalist, and thus protected by the privilege, must be determined by the person's intent at the inception of the information-gathering process. Third, an individual successfully may assert the journalist's privilege if he is involved in activities traditionally associated with the gathering and dissemination of news, even though he may not ordinarily be a member of the institutionalized press. Fourth, the relationship between the journalist and his source may be confidential or non-confidential for purposes of the privilege. Fifth, unpublished resource material likewise may be protected.[9]

Several pages later, the court again dismissed any requirement of institutional affiliation. To the contrary, the opinion quoted *Branzburg's* expansive list of others who might claim privilege—a list White had compiled as a reason to *reject* a privilege—and used it to say who might have one.

> The intended manner of dissemination may be by newspaper, magazine, book, public or private broadcast medium, handbill or the like, for "the press in its historic connotation comprehends every sort of publication which affords a vehicle of information and opinion." . . .
>
> Further, the protection from disclosure may be sought by one not traditionally associated with the institutionalized press because "the informative function asserted by representatives of the organized press . . . is also performed by lecturers, political pollsters, novelists, academic researchers, and dramatists."[10]

Reynolds lost because she had "gathered information initially for purposes other than to disseminate information to the public."[11] The intent to disseminate must exist at the inception.

The Second Circuit revisited *von Bulow* twenty-five years later in another high-profile case. Chevron went to federal court in New York to challenge the legality of an Ecuadorian court's judgment that held Texaco (which Chevron had acquired) liable for environmental damage in Ecuador. Again, we are not concerned with the legal issues in the case except one. A lower court had ordered Joseph Berlinger, a filmmaker, "to produce . . . the videotape footage constituting the outtakes" from his film *Crude*, whose subject was the Ecuador litigation.[12] On appeal, Berlinger argued that as a journalist he had a privilege to refuse to do so. Fatal to his privilege claim was the fact that Berlinger was not independent when he did this work: he had been "solicited . . . to create a documentary of the litigation from the perspective of [the] clients" of the lawyers who solicited him, and he "concededly removed at least one scene from the final version of *Crude* at their direction."[13] The court stressed, however, that solicitation from a party with an interest in the final product will not necessarily deprive a journalist of Press Clause protection. "Without doubt, such a journalist can establish entitlement to the privilege by establishing the independence of her journalistic process, for example, through evidence of editorial and financial independence."[14] Berlinger might seek to rely on the Speech Clause, which protects everyone, but not the Press Clause, which protects only the press. "The [Press Clause] privilege," the court wrote, "is designed to support the press in its valuable public service of seeking out and revealing truthful information. An undertaking to publish matter in order to promote the interests of another, regardless of justification, does not serve the same public interest, regardless of whether the resultant work may prove to be one of high quality."[15] This is as clear a recognition of a distinct role for the Press Clause as one can imagine.

The Ninth Circuit Court of Appeals, based in San Francisco, has built on the Second Circuit's analysis. In *Shoen v. Shoen* (1993), the question was whether a book author enjoyed the same First Amendment protection as did a member of the institutional press. In ruling that he did, the court used the kind of soaring language about the importance of the press that has long been missing in Supreme Court opinions. Especially noteworthy, it endorsed the importance of investigative reporting. "The journalist's privilege is designed to protect investigative reporting, regardless of the medium used to report the news to the public. Investigative book authors, like more conventional reporters, have historically played a vital role in bringing to light 'newsworthy' facts on topical and controversial matters of great public importance." The court cited Lincoln Steffens, Upton Sinclair, Rachel Carson, Ralph Nader, Jessica Mitford, and Bob Woodward as examples of authors whose books would fall within the privilege. "The critical question for deciding whether a person may invoke the journalist's privilege is whether she is gathering news for dissemination to the public."[16]

The First Circuit Court of Appeals, based in Boston, has said that the privilege also protects academic researchers. In an antitrust case, Microsoft subpoenaed "notes, tape recordings and transcripts of interviews, and correspondence with interview subjects" from two professors who had written a book. The court acknowledged that the authors were not "professional newsmen" but added:

> Courts afford journalists a measure of protection from discovery initiatives in order not to undermine their ability to gather and disseminate information. . . . The same concerns suggest that courts ought to offer similar protection to academicians engaged in scholarly research. After all, scholars too are information gatherers and disseminators. If their research materials were freely subject to subpoena, their sources likely would refuse to confide in them. As with reporters, a drying-up of sources would sharply curtail the information available to academic researchers and thus would restrict their output.[17]

The court relied on *von Bulow* and, remarkably, made no effort to reconcile its decision with *Branzburg*, which it did not mention.

The federal Freedom of Information Act (FOIA) must also define the press because it entitles "representatives of the news media" to reduced fees when requesting records. The FOIA's definition does not limit this term to the institutional press and recognizes that "editorial skills" are part of the definition:

> The term "a representative of the news media" means any person or entity that gathers information of potential interest to a segment of the public, uses its editorial skills to turn the raw materials into a distinct work, and distributes that work to an audience. In this clause, the term "news" means information that is about current events or that would be of current interest to the public. . . . A freelance journalist shall be regarded as working for a news-media entity if the journalist can demonstrate a solid basis for expecting publication through that entity, whether or not the journalist is actually employed by the entity.[18]

Apart from federal cases finding and defining a reporter's privilege and the FOIA definition of the "news media," another place to look for a definition of the press are state shield laws. These laws give journalists the right to conceal certain information received in confidence without risking contempt of court. Protection under state shield laws differs from the federal cases described earlier. The shield laws are a product of legislation, not judicial opinions interpreting the First Amendment. The scope of protection depends on the shield law that governs the question before the court. "When the *Branzburg* decision issued" in 1972, one judge has observed, "only seventeen states had recognized some protection for a reporter regarding his or her confidential sources. Today [2013], only one state, Wyoming, has not enacted or adopted a reporter's privilege. Thirty-nine states and the District of Columbia have shield laws for reporters, whether those shields are absolute or qualified."[19] Courts in ten other states have recognized a reporter's privilege in court decisions.[20]

Even though they address the same question (protection for a source's identity), the definition of the press in state shield laws is more restrictive than in many court opinions that find a qualified privilege under common law or the state or federal constitutions. Shield laws often refer to the institutional press or a person affiliated with it, rather than a broader category defined by the nature of a person's work. A partial explanation for this narrower view may be the fact that many shield laws were adopted long before the internet. New York's shield law, for example, was first adopted in 1970 and last amended in 1990. Its protection provides a shield against a finding of contempt for refusal to disclose information. The protection is absolute for "any news obtained or received in confidence or the identity of the source of any such news" and qualified for nonconfidential sources. Protected are "professional journalist[s] [and] newscaster[s] . . . employed or otherwise associated with any newspaper, magazine, wire service," or other identified media institutions.[21]

State shield laws are unavailable when federal courts enforce federal law, including federal criminal law.[22] Consequently, there have long been attempts, so far unsuccessful, to enact a federal shield law in order to protect journalists from efforts to require them to disclose confidential information in federal court. While those efforts might fail in the lower federal courts that read *Branzburg* narrowly, a future Supreme Court could overturn this anti-*Branzburg* precedent. Senate Bill 987, introduced in 2013 and labeled the "Free Flow of Information Act of 2013," is the most detailed recent attempt to create statutory federal protection. It would protect "covered journalists" from compelled disclosure of "protected information," which is defined to include the identity of a source who has been promised confidentiality and documents and records the journalist promised to keep confidential.[23] The protection is qualified. It can be overcome—for example, to prevent death, kidnapping, sexual abuse of a minor, and terrorist acts.

Of immediate interest is the definition of "covered journalist." It is broad enough to include not only employees of media companies but also independent contractors, some book authors, and bloggers. The bill's focus is not on a person's status but his or her purpose. A covered journalist must have the "primary intent to investigate events and procure material in order to disseminate to the public news or information concerning local, national, or international events or other matters of public interest." That intent must have been present at the inception of the work. The proposed law would not apply to a person who claimed that, as it happens, she just recently decided to convert what she has learned into a piece of journalism, a claim anyone can decide to make when convenient and that, if upheld, would seriously weaken judicial and legislative power to compel testimony.

If the protection given the press, from whatever source, depends on purpose, not institutional status, we need to ask whether anyone who has that purpose should enjoy the protection—be it the "lonely pamphleteer" or blogger or a *Wall Street Journal* reporter. That was one challenge facing the drafters of the Free Flow of Information Act. This may seem only a hypothetical question when it comes to investigative reporting, a question we ask to test the limits of an idea but lacking any practical implications. For how often will we see a freelance blogger doing investigative reporting? Perhaps more often than we might predict, certainly at the local level. Nor can we limit ourselves to what is true today. We should anticipate what is hereafter possible, even likely, including loose confederations of bloggers whose shifting memberships conduct serial investigations by cooperating within and across social-media platforms. Consortiums of investigators, organized to answer a single question, might form and then disband.

The category of "covered journalist" in the Free Flow of Information Act has limits. That is unavoidable. It cannot include everyone who may decide that he or she is a journalist without risking significantly limiting the protection Congress is willing to grant, if it is willing to grant any. This is why the proposition that "we are all journalists now," intended as a display of inclusiveness, is bad for journalism. Just as the Press Clause requires a legal definition of the press, a state or federal shield law requires a legal definition of a journalist. So the authors of the Free Flow of Information Act excluded, for example, the blogger just starting out, as yet on no one's payroll and without a publishing contract. A person, even if otherwise highly credentialed, who begins reporting for a nonfiction book but who has not yet sold it (or tried to sell it) is also excluded unless she was a "covered journalist" for a "continuous one-year period within the [prior] 20 years or any continuous three-month period within the 5 [prior] years." However, there is a way around the exclusions. These writers and others can get covered journalist status if a judge later decides that it "would be in the interest of justice and necessary to protect lawful and legitimate news-gathering activities" to grant it. That cannot, however, be known during the reporting, making any confidentiality promise legally uncertain. Not only prosecutors but also civil litigants may demand the information, as they did in *von Bulow* and *Chevron*. If a judge rules that the writer or researcher is not a "covered journalist," the statute would provide no protection. But uncertainty is present today in courts that recognize a qualified privilege for members of the press as they define the term.

Expressly unprotected under the proposed federal statute are persons "whose principal function . . . is to publish primary source documents that have been disclosed to such person . . . without authorization." This language is obviously aimed at "document dump" organizations, like Wikileaks, that do not exercise independent editorial judgment in deciding what to publish and so are not considered the press. In affording qualified protection against compelled disclosure, the bill expects editorial judgment in return. By doing so, it delegates to editors the responsibility and the power to disclose or withhold information depending on their view of the "public interest." Editors are, in effect, trusted to exercise a discretion generally associated with government officials.[24] If we think of the press as a fourth branch of government (though not itself part of government), then in a system of checks and balances, the bill's protection against compelled disclosure of sources bolsters the press's checking power, while the reciprocal expectation of editorial judgment acts as a check against the press's own abuse of power.

The Free Flow of Information Act would apply only in federal court, not state court. Yet Congress does have the power to extend its provisions to cases in state courts. It did just that in another law meant to protect the press. It passed the Privacy Protection Act of 1980 (PPA) to limit the effect of the Supreme Court's decision in *Zurcher v. Stanford Daily*, which upheld the search of a newspaper's office.[25] The PPA provides the press with qualified protection against searches for and seizure of work-product materials and other documents.[26] It limits federal, state, and local law-enforcement agencies and provides civil remedies if it is violated.[27] The PPA is instructive for a second reason. It easily defines the persons who were protected from government searches, based on their purpose. Any "person reasonably believed to have a purpose to disseminate to the public a newspaper, book, broadcast, or other similar form of public communication" is within the law's protection.[28]

We can now begin to identify criteria for work to fall within the Press Clause. This is the task that the Supreme Court in *Branzburg v. Hayes* decided was too hard, but it is a task many others have performed. Borrowing from them, we can say that work is within the Press Clause if it was undertaken at the outset with the primary intent to investigate events or persons and to procure material in order to disseminate to the public news or information concerning matters of public interest. The writer need not be affiliated with a newspaper or other traditional or untraditional news organization. The writer must be independent of—not subject to the control of—the subject of the work. Press Clause protection is qualified, which means a claim can be defeated if a court concludes that the interests served by disclosure are stronger by some quantum of proof than the interests served by protection. Persons or institutions claiming to fall within the coverage of the Press Clause have the burden of proving their entitlement. That proof must include the exercise of editorial judgment, which is an essential condition for the benefits the Press Clause confers, although it need not come from an editor at an institutional media organization.

One might criticize this definition on the ground that its borders are not entirely clear. True, they are not. While some work will surely qualify as within the Press Clause, and some work will surely fail to qualify, the answer for yet other work may be too close to call. For example, a writer's primary purpose when starting work may be ambiguous. The exercise of editorial judgment may be in doubt. When this sort of uncertainty happens in law, as it often does, it is left for a judge to decide the question. That's what the Free Flow of Information Act would do for the work of freelancers who lack a track record or a publishing contract. Precise language that leaves no room for judicial intervention (a daunting drafting challenge) might avoid uncertainty, but the result may be substantially to narrow the protected population. Some vagueness is not a weakness but a strength. It offers flexibility. It enables judges to apply the principles that the definition aims to enshrine in order to protect a larger group that might otherwise be excluded. That flexibility will be especially welcome as technology expands the opportunities to "do journalism" in unanticipated ways.

3

WHAT DOES THE PRESS CLAUSE DEMAND OF THE PRESS?

We recognize the Press Clause as an autonomous source of rights in part to enable the press to fulfill the important constitutional job of informing the public about government and powerful persons and institutions. In return, it must do its job in a manner that encourages our trust in the information. The generous protection of the Speech Clause remains available to all others. While the press rightly resists externally-imposed rules that presume to tell it how to do its job, internally adopted ethical standards are necessary. If the Press Clause protected everyone without regard to ethical standards, it would be redundant of the Speech Clause and count for nothing, which appears to be the current view of a majority of justices. If, instead, the Press Clause is to provide additional protection, we must describe what society gets in return. The fact that we do not and will not license the press is no impediment to expecting standards of professionalism when journalists, scholars, and authors rely on the Press Clause. Special protection has a price, which the press should embrace and help identify.

I have argued that the press is part of the American system of checks and balances—with a responsibility to report not only on each of the three branches of government at all levels but also on private institutions (including itself) and individuals. It is integral to governance, but it is not the government. A system of checks and balances presumes that, with rare exception, no power is absolute. One branch of government can check another. So we must ask: Who will check the press? The ultimate check, of course, is the judiciary. The press is not above the law. It may sound strange to make judges the final arbiters of who qualifies as the press and the benefits of membership in it. It makes the judiciary a check on organizations and individuals who serve as a check on government, including the judiciary. While this arrangement is circular, it is true today. There is no way around it consistent with the rule of law. Courts decide if an article is a basis for liability, if a newsgathering method is lawful, and if litigants have the right to question reporters or learn their sources.

What interrupts the apparent circularity of giving judges power over those who would expose official wrongdoing is judicial deference to the decisions of editors and reporters. Deference is more likely if editors and reporters work under ethical standards developed in advance, not on the fly or intuitively. Is there a document describing these standards, and what does it say? Are they the product of deliberation, applied conscientiously, and part of the training for reporters and editors? Are they periodically reviewed? Are they enforced?[1] This is not a plea for a formal code of press ethics or a professional credentialing body authorized to approve admission to (or expulsion from) Press Clause benefits. Press organizations have published ethics codes to govern the conduct of their members, and press groups like the Society of Professional Journalists have proposed model codes. Some are brief.[2] Others run to dozens of pages with examples and discussion.[3] None is legally binding. Some may demand more of reporters than the courts will require for inclusion in Press Clause protections. That's fine. The goals of a press organization can differ from Press Clause expectations. Those goals may include a particular vision for the publication's reputation (its brand).

Any criteria for status as "the press" will be imprecise, but many news organizations will easily satisfy them because their internal standards are at least as demanding. Others, including writers unaffiliated with a news organization, will find it harder to qualify. But it is certainly possible. An unaffiliated writer may follow habits of work learned as an employee at a press organization or at school. A scholar will be governed by standards of proof and accuracy expected of researchers in his or her field.

EDITORIAL (AND REPORTORIAL) JUDGMENT

Any effort to reframe the debate about the meaning of the Press Clause must recognize the centrality of editorial judgment. In an age when anyone can publish stories to the world, not every journalist will have an editor. But traditionally, journalists do have editors. Judges will defer to editors on the question of newsworthiness when the unhappy subject of a story seeks damages for invasion of privacy or when a media defendant claims that a story is entitled to greater protection against a libel claim because its subject is a matter of public concern. Justices Breyer and O'Connor, concurring in *Bart-nicki v. Vopper* (2001),[4] recognized the importance of (and respect for) editorial judgment, which may be demanded under time constraints. Editorial judgment in turn implies standards for deciding what information merits publication. It also requires rules for newsgathering. We can use the label "journalistic ethics" for these standards and rules. Journalistic ethics must be credible and honored. Courts cannot be expected to defer to editorial judgments if the rules are a mirage and the market (giving readers what they are presumed to want) is the sole consideration for publication.

RECOGNITION OF EDITORIAL JUDGMENT IN THE LOWER COURTS

Courts will defer to editorial judgment. The clearest expression of that deference occurs when a person claims that a story violates her right to privacy through the disclosure of private facts about her. Although variously articulated, a privacy claim has two components—the information disclosed must be highly offensive to a reasonable person and not of legitimate public concern. The second requirement is sometimes called newsworthiness. One federal appellate court described the privacy tort this way:

> The two criteria, offensiveness and newsworthiness, are related. An individual, and more pertinently perhaps the community, is most offended by the publication of intimate personal facts when the community has no interest in them beyond the voyeuristic thrill of penetrating the wall of privacy that surrounds a stranger.[5]

How do judges decide whether a story is newsworthy? A leading decision of the California Supreme Court[6] sought to answer this question. A single-car roadside accident caused serious injury. A television crew at the scene recorded the efforts of medical personnel to treat the victims and get them to a hospital. After the broadcast, the victims, whose images were prominent, sued for publication of private facts (i.e., invasion of privacy), among other claims. The court first addressed the issue of newsworthiness.

> Newsworthiness [is] difficult to define because it may be used as either a descriptive or a normative term. . . . A position at either extreme has unpalatable consequences. If "newsworthiness" is completely descriptive—if all coverage that sells papers or boosts ratings is deemed newsworthy—it would seem to swallow the publication of private facts tort, for it would be difficult to suppose that publishers were in the habit of reporting occurrences of little interest. At the other extreme, if newsworthiness is viewed as a purely normative concept, the courts could become to an unacceptable degree editors of the news and self-appointed guardians of public taste.[7]

The court rejected what it called a "descriptive predicate." There could then be no privacy claim for disclosure of private facts. Courts would have no role because publication would automatically establish newsworthiness. But neither did the court discount the judgment of editors. It would give

> considerable deference to reporters and editors. . . . The constitutional privilege to publish truthful material "ceases to operate only when an editor abuses his broad discretion

to publish matters that are of legitimate public interest."
By confining our interference to extreme cases, the courts
"avoid unduly limiting . . . the exercise of effective editorial judgment."[8]

How authorities respond to a serious car accident and res-
cue the victims is indeed newsworthy. No one doubted it.
The plaintiffs claimed, however, that the station's disclosures
went too far. Even if an incident is newsworthy, it does not
follow that *all* information about it is newsworthy. Who
makes that judgment? Here, too, courts will defer to editors.
The station broadcast certain information about Ruth, one of
the victims. Ruth claimed that because private information
about her was not newsworthy even if the accident was, the
broadcast invaded her privacy.

> Plaintiffs argue that showing Ruth's "intimate private,
> medical facts and her suffering was not *necessary* to enable
> the public to understand the significance of the accident
> or the rescue as a public event." The standard, however, is
> not necessity. That the broadcast *could* have been edited to
> exclude some of Ruth's words and images and still excite a
> minimum degree of viewer interest is not determinative.
> Nor is the possibility that the members of this or another
> court, or a jury, might find a differently edited broadcast
> more to their taste or even more interesting. The courts do
> not, and constitutionally could not, sit as superior editors
> of the press.[9]

This view is not unique. Similar lessons appear in other
cases. In 1984, the New York Court of Appeals, in rejecting a
defamation claim against a newspaper, wrote that state law

recognized "the need for judgment and discretion to be exercised by the journalists, subject only to review by the courts to protect against clear abuses. Determining what editorial content is of legitimate public interest and concern is a function for editors."[10] In another case, a medical journal wrote about a malpractice claim against an anesthesiologist. Its article identified the doctor's psychiatric and personal problems and implied a connection between them and the alleged malpractice. While a story about the failure to police doctor competence was certainly newsworthy, the doctor argued that the journal had no basis for implying a connection to her psychiatric history and therefore no right to reveal that history and her personal problems. That information was gratuitous, she argued. The court disagreed. "A rule forbidding editors from drawing inferences from truthful newsworthy facts," it wrote,

> would result in a far too restrictive and wholly unjustifiable construction of the first amendment privilege. If the press is to have the generous breathing space that courts have accorded it thus far, editors must have freedom to make reasonable judgments and to draw one inference where others also reasonably could be drawn.[11]

Courts recognize that the issue in these cases is not limited to the information the story discloses. Deference extends to how a journalist chooses to tell a story, which includes the choice of details to include. In the California case, Ruth argued that the television station did not need to identify the victims of the accident. What did their names or likenesses add to a story about the response to roadside accidents? The story would be the same whether the victim was named Jane or Kate or Ruth. The court disagreed.

> One might argue that . . . the images and sounds that
> potentially allowed identification of Ruth as the accident
> victim were irrelevant and of no legitimate public interest in
> a broadcast that aired some months after the accident and
> had little or no value as "hot" news. We do not take that
> view. . . . In a video documentary of this type the use of
> that degree of truthful detail would seem not only relevant,
> but essential to the narrative.[12]

The important words here are the last four: "essential to the
narrative." With these words the court deferred to editorial
judgment not only on the question of newsworthiness and
content but also on how to report the story. Detail, as every
writer knows, does things that abstract language cannot. Yes,
the broadcast might have disguised Ruth's identity by using
another name (or no name) and by obscuring her face. But an
editor might also conclude that doing so would weaken the
story—that the information was essential to the narrative—
and the court was willing to accept that judgment.[13]

Consider the more assertive recognition of the importance
of storytelling and deference to editorial judgment in *Haynes
v. Alfred A. Knopf, Inc.*[14] Nicholas Lemann, who went on to
become a *New Yorker* staff writer and dean of the Columbia
Journalism School, wrote a book called *The Promised Land:
The Great Black Migration and How It Changed America.* Its
subject is black migration from the American South in the
middle of the twentieth century. In telling that story, Lemann
used the experience of, among others, a woman name Ruby Lee
Daniels. Daniels had been married to Luther Haynes. Lemann
recounted decades-old episodes in which Haynes's behavior
toward Daniels was less than exemplary.[15] Haynes and his new
wife sued for, among other things, invasion of privacy. He

described how Lemann's disclosures had harmed him, without justification as he saw it.[16]

> The Hayneses question whether the linkage between the author's theme and their private life really is organic. They point out that many social histories do not mention individuals at all, let alone by name. That is true. Much of social science, including social history, proceeds by abstraction, aggregation, and quantification rather than by case studies. . . . But it would be absurd to suggest that cliometric or other aggregative, impersonal methods of doing social history are the only proper way to go about it and presumptuous to claim even that they are the best way. . . . Lemann's methodology places the individual case history at center stage. If he cannot tell the story of Ruby Daniels without waivers from every person who she thinks did her wrong, he cannot write this book.

The Hayneses (like Ruth in the California case) argued that there was no need to identify them by name. Their names added nothing to Lemann's story. The court rejected that argument. To obscure the Hayneses' identities, "Lemann would have had to change some, perhaps many, of the details. But then he would no longer have been writing history. He would have been writing fiction. . . . . Reporting the true facts about real people is necessary to obviate any impression that the problems raised in the [book] are remote or hypothetical."[17]

The privacy cases reveal the extent to which courts respect and protect editorial (or in the case of *The Promised Land*, authorial) judgment. The respect is not without limits. The *Haynes* court, for example, wrote that the book "does not offer the reader a titillating glimpse of tabooed activities. The tone is decorous and restrained."[18] The California court, ruling on Ruth's privacy claim, said the same when it declined to treat newsworthiness as solely a descriptive term, the meaning of which is entirely left to editors to decide with no role at all for the courts. But neither would it call newsworthiness a normative term whose meaning the courts alone decide.[19]

We see deference to editors in defamation cases, too. In 1983, *Newsweek* recapped South Dakota's nine-year effort to extradite Dennis Banks. Banks, a leader of the American Indian Movement, had participated in a 1973 riot at the courthouse in Custer, South Dakota. A year later, Banks brought charges in a tribal court against William Janklow, a South Dakota lawyer, for raping the fifteen-year-old babysitter for Janklow's children. At the time, Janklow was a candidate for state attorney general. Eight months after Banks made his charge, *Newsweek* reported in its recap, "Janklow—who had won his election despite the messy publicity—was prosecuting Banks. And his case—based on the 1973 Custer riot—was successful. Found guilty of riot and assault without intent to kill, Banks jumped bail before sentencing." Nine years later, Banks was still a fugitive.

Janklow sued *Newsweek* for libel. What was the libel? Everything in the eight-paragraph story was true. But Janklow claimed that the story implied that he "was prosecuting" Banks as revenge for Banks's rape accusation. The story omitted a critical fact. Acting as a special prosecutor, Janklow had charged Banks for the courthouse riot *before* Banks had ever accused Janklow of rape. By using the words "was prosecuting," the story made it appear that Janklow, having won the election for attorney general, then abused his new power to *initiate* a vengeful prosecution.[20] So, yes, every fact in the story was true, but the story implied a timeline that was false. The Eighth Circuit Court of Appeals in St. Louis, in a 2–1 opinion, initially ruled that Janklow (by then the governor of South Dakota) stated a valid claim.[21] But the full court reconsidered the case and dismissed the complaint in a 6–3 vote. In its opinion (also cited in the introduction), the majority wrote:

> At bottom, we face a question of usage; had *Newsweek* changed a single word and said the plaintiff *"continued prosecuting"* Banks, the implication of revenge would be more difficult to draw, and there would not even be an arguable misstatement of underlying fact. Janklow argues that it is precisely because *Newsweek* could have written a clearer sentence that the statement is actionable. We disagree. We believe that the First Amendment cautions courts against intruding too closely into questions of editorial judgment, such as the choice of specific words. Editors' grilling of reporters on word choice is a necessary aggravation. But when courts do it, there is a chilling effect on the exercise of First Amendment rights.[22]

If *Newsweek* had used the phrase "continued prosecuting," the inference of abuse of power to get revenge would indeed be "more difficult to draw." But it would remain possible. Readers might conclude that Janklow, as attorney general, chose to continue the prosecution of Banks because of the rape allegation. Through its omission, *Newsweek* strengthened the revenge inference.[23] The dissenting opinion did not disagree that a one-word change would have defeated a libel claim. But word choice, it said, is what libel is all about.

Newsweek's story was incomplete, perhaps unfair (even judges in the majority seemed to think so), and may have misled the magazine's readers. It would merit criticism if taught in a journalism class. Media ethics require fairness and accuracy. But a violation of ethical standards does not make a report legally actionable. Ethical standards should be higher than *whatever is not illegal*. So the question for the court was whether omission of a fact that would weaken, but not eliminate, a defamatory inference is a basis for a libel action against the press. In answering no, the majority opinion several times emphasized the importance of editorial judgment, including about word choice, and the need for judges to stay out of the editorial process. The court did not reject all judicial authority to review editorial judgment. Total deference to editors would place the media outside the rule of law, to which everyone is subject. The court cautioned against "intruding too closely."

A rare dramatic example of judicial refusal to defer to editorial judgment arose in the invasion-of-privacy lawsuit against *Gawker* for publishing the Hulk Hogan sex tape. After it lost, *Gawker* declared bankruptcy. The case then settled without appellate review because *Gawker* was unable to post the $50 million bond required to stay enforcement of the $140 million jury verdict.[24] So we do not know if an appellate court would have deferred to *Gawker*'s claim that the plaintiff, Terry Bollea, through his Hulk Hogan public persona, made the sex tape newsworthy.[25] We also do not know if an appellate court would have reduced the $140 million judgment to an amount that would have allowed *Gawker* to avoid bankruptcy. The argument against the tape's newsworthiness was strong. Whatever news value it had could have come in a description of its content and broadcast of less explicit parts.

But for so consequential a decision to be made by a single trial judge, with no opportunity for appellate review, is a loss for the First Amendment. Less onerous appeal terms and a stay of enforcement of the judgment could have avoided this outcome.

RECOGNITION OF EDITORIAL JUDGMENT IN THE SUPREME COURT

The Supreme Court's treatment of editorial judgment and its relationship to the First Amendment is confused. In recent years, the Court has been dismissive of the Press Clause, which makes editorial judgment legally irrelevant. If the First Amendment is only about speech, with no room for "the press" except as one more speaker, editors don't constitutionally matter. We are then all speakers or writers, and some speakers and writers happen to have editors while others do not. Those with editors might be called "the press," but legally speaking they would be just a category of speaker. The editorial filter may help ensure accuracy and compliance with a writer's own standards or those of her employer. It can prevent content that may be defamatory or otherwise actionable. But it cannot, in this view, bring the press added protection from the Press Clause.

It was not always so. In earlier decades, editorial judgment seemed like it would carry more weight in the Supreme Court. The Court displayed respect for the editorial process in cases that can only be understood as Press Clause cases, or so it then seemed. In 1973, for example, while upholding a law forbidding a newspaper to use separate male and female "help wanted" columns, the Court wrote that its decision did not authorize any restriction whatever, whether of content or layout, on stories or commentary originated by Pittsburgh Press, its columnists, or its contributors. On the contrary, we reaffirm unequivocally the protection afforded to editorial judgment and to the free expression of views on these and other issues, however controversial.[26]

In the same opinion, the Court recognized the needs of the "institutional" press. "This is not a case," it wrote, "in which the challenged law arguably disables the press by undermining its institutional viability. . . . The Court has recognized on several occasions the special institutional needs of a vigorous press by striking down laws taxing the advertising revenue of newspapers with circulations in excess of 20,000 . . . requiring a license for the distribution of printed matter . . . and prohibiting the door-to-door distribution of leaflets."[27]

Also in 1973, the Court rejected a request from the Democratic National Committee for a ruling that "under the First Amendment . . . a broadcaster may not, as a general policy, refuse to sell time to responsible entities . . . for the solicitation of funds and for comment on public issues."[28] Chief Justice Burger wrote:

It would be anomalous for us to hold, in the name of promoting the constitutional guarantees of free expression, that the day-to-day editorial decisions of broadcast licensees are subject to the kind of restraints urged by [the Democratic National Committee]. To do so in the name of the First Amendment would be a contradiction. . . . [29]

For better or worse, *editing is what editors are for*; and editing is selection and choice of material. That editors—newspaper or broadcast—can and do abuse this power is beyond doubt, but that is no reason to deny the discretion Congress provided. Calculated risks of abuse are taken in order to preserve higher values.[30]

In 1974, the Court addressed the constitutionality of a Florida "compulsory access law," which required newspapers to publish without charge the reply of a candidate for political office who claims that a story "assailed . . . his personal character or official record." A unanimous Court found the law unconstitutional, citing protection for "editorial control and judgment" and questioning "how governmental regulation of this crucial process can be exercised consistent with First Amendment guarantees of a free press as they have evolved to this time."[31]

The "Florida statute," the Court wrote, "fails to clear the barriers of the First Amendment because of its intrusion into the function of editors. . . . The choice of material to go into a newspaper, and the decisions made as to limitations on the size and content of the paper, and treatment of public issues and public officials—whether fair or unfair—constitute the exercise of *editorial control and judgment*."[32]

That is about as far as the Court has been willing to go in recognizing the role of editors under the First Amendment. We cannot say that the Court would go even this far today. It certainly hasn't followed these pronouncements to their logical conclusion. But assuming that the Court would repeat them (because doing so is easy and entails no commitment), here is all we can fairly conclude about how the Court thinks of editorial judgment. Editorial judgment means: *Don't tell the press what to say or not to say or how to say it.* That may be satisfying, but it is also inadequate. The Court does not need the Press Clause and the presence of editors to say "hands off" the press; it can say the same under the Speech Clause. The government cannot tell speakers what to say, what not to say, or how to say it. The upshot is that editorial judgment would then confer no protection denied everyone else. While the fact of editorial judgment implies the existence of the press as a *practical* matter, as a legal matter editorial judgment would change nothing. Or perhaps we can say a bit more. In the Court's equivocal world, cases that seek to protect editorial judgment both are and are not Press Clause cases. They are Press Clause cases because in ruling that the press may not be told what to write or broadcast, the Court cites editorial judgment, but they are not Press Clause cases because they would be decided the same way under the Speech Clause without ever mentioning editors or the press.

The Court's equivocation (the most optimistic way to put it) sacrifices something valuable. Here were opportunities (partially) to define those whom the Press Clause protects and how it does so. A distinct role for the Press Clause in First Amendment jurisprudence would recognize the importance of editorial and reportorial judgment, which can transform raw material into a book, article, or broadcast into something that we identify as new and deserving of enhanced legal protection. A requirement of reportorial and editorial judgment for Press Clause protection would exclude works that lack them. It would exclude "document dumps." Wikileaks is not the press. Stories in the *Guardian* and the *Washington Post*, filtering Edward Snowden's disclosures or the Panama Papers (or even documents from Wikileaks) through editors and additional reporting, are the press.

My argument for a reinvigorated Press Clause depends on judicial respect for editorial judgment, but there must be editorial judgment in fact. That means that courts will be delegating power to unelected editors,[33] which may seem counterintuitive, even undemocratic. The courts' willingness to defer to editors will expand or contract as judicial confidence in the way the press makes decisions and reports stories increases or shrinks. Properly viewed, the cases in which judges defer to editorial judgment are Press Clause cases, not Speech Clause cases. Editorial judgment is a hallmark of the press. Everyone can speak and write, but not all speakers and writers have editors or exercise editorial judgment.[34]

Satisfaction of an editorial-judgment requirement for Press Clause protection will ordinarily be easy if the writer is affiliated with a press organization and has an editor (or several). But it will be harder if the writer is the not-so-hypothetical lonely blogger, the present-day equivalent of the "lonely pamphleteer" whom Justice White evoked in rejecting "a constitutional newsman's privilege" in *Branzburg*.[35] A solitary blogger will not have an editor. Book authors and academic researchers may lack the degree of editorial oversight that journalists receive. These differences are not fatal. The burden to establish entitlement to the benefits that the Press Clause confers falls on the person claiming them. The burden will be easier for the legacy press to satisfy but is not insurmountable for others. Scholars, for example, work under the standards for accuracy and fairness imposed by their field of study. The question will be whether the writers perform for themselves, possibly with editorial guidance or collegial advice, the job that editors traditionally do for reporters.

What is that job? My aim is to protect investigative reporting as a check on harmful (including illegal) conduct by public and private actors. Imagine an investigation that turns up information tending to reveal such behavior. Maybe the publication got the information in part through a tip or unauthorized leak, maybe through deception (discussed below), or maybe through an act that the law calls trespass (see chapter 5). Most likely the story is the product of deeply reported enterprise journalism. The editorial job now requires deliberation, thinking through. It demands mindfulness. It entails balancing the public interest in disclosure against harm to the public interest or to individuals from disclosure, doing so first for the story as a whole and then for each part of it. What information should go in and what should not? Are the facts true? These are decisions that the subjects of a story could make if they had retained control of the information. But self-interest will dispose them toward concealment. A writer and editor, on the other hand, may be professionally and commercially disposed toward disclosure and quick to dismiss contrary arguments. Yet once they have managed to get the information, it is the writer and editor who get to decide, and courts will defer (but not capitulate) to an actual exercise of discretion.

It may seem odd that authority to decide whether to disclose information will shift to the press from the person or entity that had the legal right, or at least the power and perhaps even the duty, to conceal it. A rule of law that delegates power to disclose to private editorial judgment with deference from—indeed the legal protection of—the state (or the courts) is extraordinary. The editor may work for a profit-making organization, introducing a financial incentive to choose to expose. Even if there is no financial inducement, disclosure may enhance reputations and lead to prizes. The editor is not elected. She has no *legal* duty to the public, which neither chose her nor can remove her. Her professional responsibility is to publish in the public interest, but the public interest as *she* conceives it. There is no appeal from her decision to publish unless it is to a superior editor within the same organization. The state, including its judiciary, is shut out of the prepublication editorial process. Despite the Supreme Court's recent reluctance to give any independent content to the Press Clause, this delegation of power to editorial judgment must rely on that clause, not the Speech Clause. The sequence of events from identifying the story, to newsgathering, to deciding how to tell the story, to editing it, to publication describes tasks historically associated with the work of the press, institutional or otherwise, not speech alone. Pretending otherwise is willful ignorance.

How to deal with writers unaffiliated with the institutional press and lacking traditional editors deserves further attention. It is not an easy issue. Limiting Press Clause status to the institutional press would make line drawing and predictions easier. But we would then exclude freelancers, bloggers, book authors, nascent periodicals, and academic researchers, notwithstanding that they may produce important work, scrupulously observe high ethical standards, and do for themselves what editors do for reporters at traditional news organizations. So a requirement of an institutional structure with editorial oversight should not be necessary for a person to qualify for Press Clause protection. Whether she does qualify will depend on the details. The stalled Free Flow of Information Act would leave it to judges to decide whether, for certain unaffiliated journalists, "protections [under the statute] would be in the interest of justice and necessary to protect lawful and legitimate news-gathering activities under the specific circumstances of the case."[36] The Press Clause can be read to do the same without need for an authorizing statute.

ACCURACY AND CORRECTION

Accuracy is essential to the press's checking function. A commitment to accuracy promotes confidence in the truth of the reported facts. Required are methods of work that will encourage accuracy and a policy of correction when mistakes nevertheless occur, as they will. Persistent negligence or persistent failures to correct errors and revisit policies to avoid recurrence mean the publication or writer is not fulfilling the checking function and should not enjoy the additional benefits of the Press Clause. The Statement of Principles of the American Society of News Editors (ASNE) puts it this way: "Good faith with the reader is the foundation of good journalism. Every effort must be made to assure that the news content is accurate, free from bias and in context, and that all sides are presented fairly." Here, again, is where editorial judgment is critical. Ensuring accuracy can take time, which may mean holding a story until all facts can be confirmed. But the public interest may counsel quicker publication. Someone has to do that balancing.

COMPLETENESS

Completeness, or thoroughness, is tied to accuracy but goes beyond it. A story may be accurate so far as it goes yet still be incomplete and distort through omission. Completeness requires giving subjects an opportunity to respond to factual statements about them, especially critical ones. But it also requires inclusion of facts or context that, for some readers or listeners, could reasonably put the story in a different light.

"Stories delivered without the context to fully understand them are incomplete," says NPR's Ethics Handbook.

FAIRNESS

"Fair" may be an overused word, but it is apt here. Fairness requires accuracy, completeness, and something more. NPR defines fairness as telling "the truest story possible." Fairness can be compromised by word choice (using words with a pejorative or laudatory connotation) or by how the story is organized, for example, the sequence in which facts are revealed. Fairness does not foreclose a point of view. But it does require honesty about facts that may challenge that point of view. It also requires giving the subject of a story a timely chance to respond to the story's statements about her. Fairness, along with accuracy and completeness, enables the reader to form her own opinion.

INDEPENDENCE

The ASNE Statement of Principles says that the "American press was made free not just to inform or just to serve as a forum for debate but also to bring an independent scrutiny to bear on the forces of power in the society, including the conduct of official power at all levels of government." The key word is "independent." It does not mean that writers and editors can have no views, that they are merely the neutral and fair transmitters of information. "Independent" refers to methodology and insulation against external influence, not perspective.

Independence imposes two requirements. First, a writer should be independent of the subjects of his story and of others who may have an interest in the story. That requires more than the absence of legal obligations to others. The writer should be free of a sense of personal obligation to others in how he reports and writes the story. The writer must have no financial or proprietary interest that threatens to distort the story. His sole loyalty is to the public, and all decisions must be made from that perspective.

The second meaning of independence concerns appearances. Lawyers and judges, when presented with disabling conflicts, will often insist that they would never *in fact* deviate from their duty. This may be true. It will, let us stipulate, usually be true. But it is equally important that the work *appear* to have been done free of the conflicting interest. Sometimes the conflicting interest (if known) may cause those for whom the work is done—here the public—to see too great a risk to the integrity of the work, despite the best intentions. Rather than ask later whether there is reason to believe that the conflict affected the work in fact (and the journalist may not be the best judge of that), it is better not to undertake the assignment in the first place. The conflict analysis must be objective and performed from the perspective of fair-minded members of the public. At the same time, where reasonable minds can differ, it may suffice to disclose the conflicting interests in the story itself. Independence and the appearance of independence demand a partition between the news side and the business side of the organization, which of course includes denying advertisers editorial influence. The publication's own business interests cannot influence content. Any cooperation with advertisers in the production of news about or affecting them must be forbidden unless disclosed, in which case it fails the checking function. A comparison to lawyers, though imperfect, may be helpful. Lawyers represent clients and advocate for a client's interests, not their own. Rules limit how they can do so. Conventionally, these are called rules of ethics or rules of professional conduct. For journalists, the public interest, as they see it, is the equivalent of the client. I write "as they see it" because unlike lawyers, journalists have no client to instruct them. They and their editors identify the public interest.[37] While there will be sharp disagreement on what that interest is or requires, reporters and editors cannot in any event pursue their own interests or those of their employer. Indeed, if a reporter's private interests could interfere with identification of the public interest, she should not be reporting the story, just as lawyers should not be representing clients if their private interests could get in the way. They would not be independent.

OTHER ETHICS CODE PROVISIONS

Some other rules in codes of media ethics can be ignored here. It is not necessary that the writer be impartial so long as she does not feign impartiality, exercises editorial judgment (or someone does it for her), and is accurate, fair, independent, and complete. Nor does she need to conceal her partiality. Abstention from partisan activity, like publicly supporting a political candidate or joining a protest march, is not required. One might even argue that a story can better serve the Press Clause if writers and editors disclose their partiality where it exists. A reader aware or informed of a reporter's bias may be skeptical of the reporting. Or not. It is just additional true information.

The analogy is not to the work of judges, for whom impartiality and the appearance of impartiality are critical.[38] While some journalism codes may choose to require the same level of impartiality from reporters and editors as we require of judges, that should not be a condition for Press Clause protection. We can trust the argument of a partial but independent author, whose viewpoint is evident, if we can trust his or her methodology and if the work is otherwise fair and complete.[39] Media organizations may prefer that their reporters appear to have no policy preferences on the subject of their stories. Many consider the appearance of agnosticism vital to their role. That is understandable, but it is not a Press Clause requirement. If it were, journals of opinion that publish investigative stories—the *Nation* or the *National Review*, for example—and many investigations that appear only online would not count as the press. Books that are not straight reportage would not qualify. Much academic research would not qualify. As long as these publications honor the conditions listed here for inclusion in the Press Clause, neither a show of detachment nor detachment in fact is needed.

Nor is a prohibition on deception in newsgathering required. This may be surprising. Ethics codes routinely say otherwise. The *New York Times'* Policy on Ethics in Journalism says that "staff members should disclose their identity to people they cover (whether face to face or otherwise), though they need not always announce their status as journalists when seeking information normally available to the public."[40] The Society of Professional Journalists envisions that deception will be justified only on rare occasions: "Avoid undercover or other surreptitious methods of gathering information unless traditional, open methods will not yield information vital to the public." NPR forbids hidden microphones except "in the very rarest of circumstances." ProPublica's code warns: "We don't misidentify or misrepresent ourselves to get a story. When we seek an interview, we identify ourselves as Pro-Publica journalists." [41] It can make good business sense for established news organizations to forbid deception. I don't question that policy. But as I argue in chapter 5, the Press Clause should protect some newsgathering that relies on deception or similar conduct.

A news organization may legitimately impose other restrictions on how its staff works or even behaves in their public or private lives, restrictions that, unlike accuracy and completeness, do not directly affect the content of what they write. Doing so may be seen to encourage public trust and the appearance (if not the fact) of neutrality and enhance a publication's reputation as an honest source of reliable information. But the question posed here is narrow: What qualities do we want in the reporting and writing of a story in order for it to serve the press's checking function? If the story is complete, accurate, and fair, if there is a policy of correction, if the writer and editor are independent, and if all decisions leading to publication reflect the operation of editorial judgment, the story will come under the protection of the Press Clause.

4

PROTECTION OF
CONFIDENTIAL INFORMATION

The Supreme Court's treatment of a reporter's privilege to protect confidential information (especially a reporter's sources) tells a story of confusion and dissimulation. Because this history is told in judicial opinions, with their many citations and the particular (sometimes opaque) conventions of judicial discourse, all but media lawyers may give up trying to understand them. But the effort will pay off. Some lower federal courts, largely ignoring the Supreme Court's *Branzburg* decision,[1] have figured out how to define the press of the Press Clause and then recognize a qualified privilege to protect confidential sources when the party seeking the information is not, as in *Branzburg*, a grand jury. Here, we turn to the Supreme Court's treatment of the issue. But it may not make strategic sense quite yet to ask the Court to revisit its troubled forty-six-year-old precedent.

The oddest feature of the denial of a reporter's privilege is the standoff to which it may lead and has led in practice. Say a federal prosecutor subpoenas a reporter and asks for the source of information in a story. Assume the reporter declines to answer, citing privilege. But then assume the court rejects the claim of privilege. The reporter will be required to comply with the subpoena or risk jail. If she identifies her source, the threat of jail will have accomplished its goal. But for reporters who choose jail over disclosure, the party who subpoenaed the reporter does not get what it wants. It is no better off. The reporter meanwhile sits in jail. We have created a set of rules whose effect, if not its purpose, will be to jail journalists who will not break confidentiality promises. True, as a matter of discretion prosecutors will often choose not to subpoena a reporter when they can get the same information elsewhere. But threats to jail reporters can and do happen. Some journalists will go to jail rather than disclose a source, unless someone blinks and the impasse is avoided. As we will see presently, a special prosecutor appointed by the second Bush administration subpoenaed and then jailed the *New York Times* reporter Judith Miller when in 2005 she refused to disclose the identity of a person who told her that Valerie Plame worked for the CIA, which was a government secret; and in 2013 the Obama administration stood ready to jail James Risen, also a *New York Times* reporter, after he refused to reveal his source for classified information regarding the Iranian nuclear weapons program, which he had disclosed in a book. In 2017, the Justice Department pledged to investigate and prosecute unauthorized White House leaks.[2] That effort could yet lead to subpoenas to reporters to disclose their sources.

Subpoenas to reporters burden the press even if the focus is not the identity of a confidential source. For example, a litigant might seek to learn what a *non*confidential source told a reporter beyond what the reporter included in a story. If the story is broadcast, the litigant might seek outtakes. The litigant might be curious to know what information a reporter could have included in a story but as it happens did not. A variation on this issue arises if a litigant wants a reporter to testify that attributed quotes she published or broadcast are accurate. Because the sources in these examples were not promised confidentiality, the reporter can't argue that compliance will affect her ability to gather news. Her weaker claim is that the time required to comply with subpoenas will interfere with her ability to do her job, much more so than it would for others. Information is what the press gathers, making reporters an attractive source of evidence for lawyers.

Few reporters will ever be forced to choose between disclosure and jail, but the way we resolve the question when it does arise will profoundly affect the press's checking function. Sources with newsworthy information are more likely to disclose it to a reporter if they know that she has a legal right to refuse to reveal her source. A legal right is better insurance than a reporter's promise. And if there is no legal right, the opposite is true. Some sources will be reluctant to trust a promise. The government will be especially interested in learning a reporter's source when a story casts doubt on the competence or integrity of government.

Understanding the *Branzburg* line of cases, which requires a dive into what may seem (because it sometimes is) legal arcana, is critical to any discussion of the Press Clause and the role of the press in American society. It is important to remember that *Branzburg* is nothing more than a pronouncement of a public policy in legal attire. It was not inevitable. It reflects a choice. *Branzburg* is said to have held that reporters have the same obligation as anyone else to respond to grand jury subpoenas—or even all subpoenas—and give evidence. I write "is said to have held" because I will challenge the accuracy of this common characterization of the case.

The Court has not, however, reconsidered *Branzburg*. Instead, it and others continue to misread it.

Branzburg resolved three different cases involving three different reporters. In each, a prosecutor investigating a crime wanted the reporter to disclose the identity of a confidential source to a grand jury. Unlike cases discussed later in this chapter, these weren't leak cases. The distinction is important. The prosecutors were *not* looking to prosecute a person for giving, or leaking, classified or other legally protected information to a reporter. The government did not claim that the source acted illegally in talking to the reporter. Rather, the prosecutors in the *Branzburg* cases wanted to know a reporter's source to help prove other crimes. Imagine, for example, that after a gangland killing, a story reports details of the crime, relying in part on a confidential source, perhaps a witness who is not a suspect but who fears retribution if she is publicly identified. The government might subpoena the reporter to learn the witness's identity, interview her, and possibly require her to testify.

Two of the cases before the Supreme Court in *Branzburg* were drug cases. In the third case, the government was seeking information about the Black Panther Party. Four justices wrote four opinions. Justice White wrote an opinion for himself, Chief Justice Burger, and Justices Blackmun and Rehnquist. Justice Powell wrote an opinion for himself but listed himself as "concurring" in the White opinion, thereby providing that opinion with the fifth vote needed to make it the opinion of the Court. But what Justice Powell wrote, and his use of the word "concurring," has made the meaning of *Branzburg* unstable in the view of many, including members of the Court. Justice Stewart wrote a dissent in which Justices Brennan and Marshall joined. Justice Douglas wrote his own dissent. This 4–1, 3–1 division among the justices has caused confusion for decades and still does.

Contributing to *Branzburg*'s instability is the fact that Justice White did not entirely dismiss the press's First Amendment claim of protection for newsgathering. Or so it seemed at the time. "We do not question the significance of free speech, press, or assembly to the country's welfare," White wrote. "Nor is it suggested that news gathering does not qualify for First Amendment protection; without some protection for seeking out the news, freedom of the press could be eviscerated."[3] Not only does this sentence purport to protect newsgathering; it also identifies freedom of the press as a distinct First Amendment concern. Later in the opinion, White again wrote that "news gathering is not without its First Amendment protections."[4] (White likely came to regret even this morsel of protection.) The protection did not extend, however, to the identity of a reporter's confidential source when demanded by a grand jury. "The *sole* issue before us is the obligation of reporters to respond to grand jury subpoenas as other citizens do and to answer questions relevant to an investigation into the commission of crime."[5] Later, the Court ignored that pesky word "sole" when it desired *Branzburg* to stand for more than it actually decided. Still later, Chief Justice Burger tried to repudiate any notion that the First Amendment protected newsgathering in any way whatsoever. More disturbing, the Court and some lower courts have treated Powell's "concurring" opinion as meaningless, as though it wasn't there, just a personal essay. Powell's later insistence that *Branzburg* had to be read in light of what he, a necessary fifth vote, had written has been ignored.

Before we get to that, consider what Powell and the dissenting justices actually said in *Branzburg*. Where White offered only a vague sentence about First Amendment protection for newsgathering, Powell wrote that the courts should "balance" press interests against the interest of a party seeking to learn the reporter's source. He used the word "balance" or "balancing" six times in three paragraphs and a footnote. He wrote:

> The asserted claim to privilege should be judged on its facts by the striking of a proper balance between freedom of the press and the obligation of all citizens to give relevant testimony with respect to criminal conduct. The balance of these vital constitutional and societal interests on a case-by-case basis accords with the tried and traditional way of adjudicating such questions.[6]

Powell assumed that the balance would be more favorable to a reporter than it would be to "all citizens" who seek to quash a subpoena because "freedom of the press" is one of the two "vital constitutional and societal interests" at stake. The other is prosecuting crime.[7] By contrast, Justice White and the three other justices who joined his opinion did not subscribe to balancing at all. The word is absent from the White opinion. What, then, of the four dissenting justices? Not only did the dissenters grant journalists greater protection than did the White opinion; they also gave the press more protection than did Powell.

Three of the justices in dissent, in an opinion by Justice Stewart, a former college journalist, laid out a balancing test aimed at protecting the press:

> Accordingly, when a reporter is asked to appear before a grand jury and reveal confidences, I would hold that the

government must (1) show that there is probable cause to believe that the newsman has information that is clearly relevant to a specific probable violation of law; (2) demonstrate that the information sought cannot be obtained by alternative means less destructive of First Amendment rights; and (3) demonstrate a compelling and overriding interest in the information.[8]

If we add the "Stewart three" to the "Powell one," we get four justices who favor balancing of competing interests and four who do not. (Justice Douglas, who also dissented, would be the tiebreaker. We come to him next.) Why didn't these four justices join in one opinion that favored balancing? How does Powell's view differ from Stewart's? Not by much. Like Powell, Stewart would recognize a qualified privilege for a reporter to refuse to reveal a source's identity to a grand jury. Like Powell, he would have the Court balance the competing interests to decide if the privilege applied. However, unlike Powell, in "very rare circumstances," Stewart would spare the reporter from even having to appear before the grand jury and claim a privilege if doing so "would substantially impair his news-gathering function." One of the three *Branzburg* cases presented just such a rare circumstance. The lower court had found that the "confidential relationship" between the *New York Times* reporter Earl Caldwell and "the leaders of the Black Panther Party would be impaired if he appeared before the grand jury at all to answer questions, even though not privileged." It added that the "very appearance by Caldwell before the grand jury would jeopardize his relationship with his sources, leading to a severance of the news-gathering relationship and impairment of the flow of news to the public."[9] Stewart agreed.[10]

At this point, we have a tie vote (4–4) on whether a court, asked to enforce a grand jury subpoena to a reporter, should or should not balance the effect on newsgathering against the need for the reporter's information. Enter Justice Douglas. In a separate dissent, Douglas was the most protective of the press. He would have recognized a reporter's absolute right not to appear before a grand jury unless the reporter himself was implicated in a crime, in which case the reporter would be able to claim his Fifth Amendment privilege against self-incrimination and refuse to appear for *that* reason. A reporter's immunity, Douglas wrote, "is therefore quite complete, for, absent his involvement in a crime, the First Amendment protects him against an appearance before a grand jury and if he is involved in a crime, the Fifth Amendment stands as a barrier."[11]

To recap: Four justices (in an opinion by White) would treat reporters the same as everyone else when subpoenaed by a grand jury. But five justices would give reporters greater protection. One justice (Powell) would give reporters heightened protection through "balancing" but only after they respond to a subpoena. Because Powell voted to enforce the subpoenas to the three reporters in *Branzburg*, we know that he struck the balance against the reporters on the facts of their particular cases. Three justices (in an opinion by Stewart) would "in very rare circumstances" relieve a reporter from even having to appear in response to a subpoena and would balance the competing interests for all others. One justice (Douglas) would recognize an absolute right not to respond to the subpoena. It would seem, then, that the correct reading of *Branzburg* should be, first, that the three reporters lost only because of how Powell weighed the balance in their particular situations; second, that balancing (and journalism) won a majority of the Court; and third, in any event, the Court's decision applies only to grand jury subpoenas.

This is not, however, how *Branzburg* is remembered. The fact that Justice Powell labeled his opinion as "concurring" has been used ever since to silence him, precedentially speaking. In this view, "concurring" is interpreted to mean that Powell agreed with every word Justice White wrote regardless of what Powell actually wrote at the time or thereafter. Powell reiterated his *Branzburg* view two years later, in a case called *Saxbe v. Washington Post Co.*[12] The *Post* had challenged a Federal Bureau of the Prisons "regulation [that] prohibited any personal interviews between newsmen and individually designated federal prison inmates."[13] This was not a confidential-source case. A 5–4 opinion by Justice Stewart upheld the regulation. Stewart said that the press was not entitled to any greater right to visit prisons than is the general public. Besides, he added, Bureau policy did in fact give the press a greater right. Among other things, the policy "permits press representatives to tour the prisons and to photograph any prison facilities. During such tours a newsman is permitted to conduct brief interviews with any inmates he might encounter."[14]

In dissent, Powell first agreed that "newsmen" have no broader rights than anyone else. "I agree, of course, that neither any news organization nor reporters *as individuals* have constitutional rights superior to those enjoyed by ordinary citizens."[15] But if reporters don't have rights superior to others, why do they get special access to prisons? Powell went on to explain that the press works for the public. "The underlying right is the right of the public generally. The press is the necessary representative of the public's interest in this context and the instrumentality [that] effects the public's right."[16]

Most important for the present discussion was Powell's reading of *Branzburg*.

> Nor does Branzburg v. Hayes compel the majority's resolution of this case. . . . The Court did not hold that the government is wholly free to restrict *press* access to newsworthy information. . . . And *I emphasized the limited nature of the Branzburg holding in my concurring opinion*. . . . A fair reading of the majority's analysis in Branzburg makes plain that the result hinged on *an assessment of the competing societal interests involved in that case.*[17]

After *Branzburg*, press organizations, their lawyers, and their supporters put great reliance not only on Powell's concurrence but also on the sliver of protection *Branzburg* appeared to allow when Justice White wrote that "news gathering is not without its First Amendment protections." Optimism soon died. In 1978, six years after *Branzburg*, a three-justice plurality that included Justice White sought to expunge that sliver. *Houchins v. KQED, Inc.*[18] addressed efforts by a television and radio station operator to gain access to a jail where an inmate had committed suicide. A lower court had issued a preliminary injunction in favor of the station. The Supreme Court reversed. The plurality, in an opinion by Chief Justice Burger, called *Branzburg*'s reference to newsgathering "dictum."[19] This is the Court's way of whiting out something it previously said. Burger is telling us that since *Branzburg* would have been decided the same way without White's reference to newsgathering, the reference to newsgathering meant nothing, legally speaking. That would certainly have been a surprise to lawyers at the time. Burger's dismissal of *Branzburg*'s newsgathering reference as dictum is less than forthright. The Court, when convenient, often relies on language from prior decisions even when the language was not strictly necessary to the ruling in those cases.

More remarkable still is that only two justices joined Burger's plurality opinion. (Two other justices did not participate.) Justice Stevens dissented in an opinion joined by Justices Powell and Brennan. Stevens found the lower court's injunctive relief appropriate. He cited Powell's dissent in *Saxbe v. Washington Post*, with its embrace of balancing, five times. And he also emphasized the need for special protection for the press, not in its own right but, as Powell did, as a representative of the public.

> Without some protection for the acquisition of information about the operation of public institutions such as prisons by the public at large, the process of self-governance contemplated by the Framers would be stripped of its substance.
>
> For that reason information gathering is entitled to some measure of constitutional protection. . . . This protection is not for the private benefit of those who might qualify as representatives of the "press" but to insure that the citizens are fully informed regarding matters of public interest and importance.[20]

So far, we have a 3–3 vote. This time, Justice Stewart was the tiebreaker, but for technical reasons he concurred in the result. He believed that the wording of the lower court's injunction was too broad. Yet his concurrence cited his own dissent in *Branzburg* (which endorsed balancing) and objected to the Burger plurality's failure to recognize an independent role for the Press Clause:

That the First Amendment speaks separately of freedom
of speech and freedom of the press is no constitutional
accident, but an acknowledgment of the critical role
played by the press in American society. The Constitution
requires sensitivity to that role, and to the special needs of
the press in performing it effectively.[21]

The vote in *Houchins* was 4 to 3 in *favor* of an independent
role for the Press Clause and for prison access by the press as
agents of the public on a properly worded injunction. Burger's
statement that *Branzburg*'s protection for newsgathering was
dictum was the losing position.

The Court has not owned up to this history. Instead, in
1990, in a case having nothing at all to do with the press, it
read *Branzburg* to "reject the notion" that the First Amendment prohibited requiring a reporter "to testify as to information obtained in confidence without a special showing
that the reporter's testimony was necessary."[22] This characterization of *Branzburg* is certainly dictum and of no precedential value. It is also wrong if Justice Powell's concurrence
means what he said it means and which he repeated in later
opinions. And it is wrong for a second reason. Even if White's
opinion in *Branzburg* is treated as an opinion for the Court,
the "sole" issue in the case, as White wrote, was the enforce-
ability of grand jury subpoenas to reporters. *Branzburg* did
not "reject" a showing of necessity for any other subpoenas,
whether from a prosecutor, a defense lawyer, or a party to a
civil lawsuit. But by 1990, Justices Douglas, Stewart, and
Powell were off the Court.

Despite *Branzburg*'s supposed rejection of a constitutional
privilege to refuse to disclose confidential sources to a grand
jury—or in the view of some, rejection of a reporter's privilege

in all circumstances—we saw in chapter 2 that a majority of lower federal appellate courts that have addressed the question has ignored a broad reading of *Branzburg* and upheld a qualified privilege anyway. As a result, any federal protection for the identity of a source will depend on which federal court hears the appeal. For their part, state courts may or may not grant broader protection based on a state constitutional or common-law privilege or under state shield laws. We lack a national rule even though many journalists work across state borders and their stories are accessible nationwide. A journalist who never leaves her home state may be subpoenaed to testify in connection with a case in a distant courtroom.

In a 2003 opinion for the Seventh Circuit Court of Appeals in Chicago,[23] Richard Posner, who has recognized no constitutional or common-law privilege under any circumstances, and who believes that *Branzburg* agrees,[24] summarized the disparate decisions:

> A large number of cases conclude, rather surprisingly in light of *Branzburg*, that there is a reporter's privilege, though they do not agree on its scope. . . .
> Some of the cases that recognize the privilege essentially ignore *Branzburg*; some treat the "majority" opinion in *Branzburg* as actually just a plurality opinion; some audaciously declare that *Branzburg* actually created a reporter's privilege. The approaches that these decisions take to the issue of privilege can certainly be questioned.

In a later case, Posner wrote that "the news media conduct investigations, and their ability to do so would be enhanced if they were permitted to conceal the identity of their sources from the government. But they are not."[25] Is Posner's reading of *Branzburg* correct? No, it is not. Not when *Branzburg* was decided, and not in light of later events. The "sole" issue in *Branzburg*, it bears repeating, was whether reporters must respond to grand jury subpoenas, but Posner ignored the word "sole."[26]

The opinions enforcing subpoenas to Judith Miller, Matthew Cooper, and James Risen illustrate the diversity of judicial views on both a constitutional and a common-law reporter's privilege even when subpoenas issue from a grand jury, as they did in *Branzburg*. These cases will help us work through the legal and policy questions. And the separate views of some of the judges can provide the intellectual scaffolding for an eventual challenge, in court or in Congress, to *Branzburg* itself.

The subpoenas to Miller and Cooper followed the public disclosure, apparently as political retaliation, that Valerie Plame was a covert CIA agent.[27] The alleged retaliation followed an op-ed in the *New York Times* by Plame's husband, Joseph Wilson. Following a trip to Niger, Wilson wrote that Saddam Hussein had not tried to obtain ingredients for nuclear weapons from sources there. The George W. Bush administration had claimed otherwise in defending the invasion of Iraq. Miller never wrote about Plame. Cooper did, but only after the columnist Robert Novak had publicly disclosed her status. Both Miller and Cooper (along with *Time*, Cooper's employer) were subpoenaed to a grand jury and ordered to provide the identity of the person who had revealed Plame's CIA status to them. This was a "leak" investigation, which means that the alleged crime was the disclosure of Plame's CIA affiliation. The Justice Department appointed a special counsel to discover and possibly prosecute the leaker or leakers. The federal appeals court in Washington, D.C., refused to quash the subpoenas. Three judges gave three different explanations. All rejected the reporters' First Amendment claim, citing *Branzburg*. But that's where their agreement ended. In Judge Sentelle's view, *Branzburg* also foreclosed a common law (i.e., judicially created, nonconstitutional) privilege for the identity of confidential sources. Judge Henderson did not agree that *Branzburg* foreclosed a common-law privilege, but she wrote that it was unnecessary to decide that question because even if there were a common-law privilege, it would be qualified, not absolute, and would be rejected in the case before the court—that is, a grand jury subpoena in the context of a leak investigation. Judge Tatel wrote that it *was* necessary to decide whether a qualified common-law privilege existed and to determine its scope. Until the scope of any common-law privilege was defined, he wrote, the court could not say whether the prosecutor's need for Miller's and Cooper's testimony was great enough to defeat the common-law privilege. Judge Tatel then recognized a qualified common-law privilege for a reporter to resist a grand jury subpoena. But on the facts before him, he concluded that the common-law privilege was unavailable.[28]

Of interest here are the factors Judges Henderson and Tatel said could either defeat or sustain a qualified common-law privilege claim—if one existed (Henderson) or which did exist (Tatel). Their views on this question may influence Congress and other courts. For Judge Henderson, the only two factors to consider were the prosecutor's need for the information and whether it was available from other sources.[29] "I am not convinced," she wrote, "that a balancing test that requires more than an evaluation of the essentiality of the information to the prosecution and the exhaustion of available alternative sources thereof is either useful or appropriate."[30] Judge Tatel opted for the more extensive balancing test Henderson rejected. To Henderson's two factors he added "the harmfulness of the leaked information and the damage to newsgathering that might flow from enforcing the disputed subpoenas."[31]

> In leak cases . . . courts applying the privilege must consider not only the government's need for the information and exhaustion of alternative sources [i.e., Judge Henderson's two factors], but also the two competing public interests lying at the heart of the balancing test. Specifically, the court must weigh the public interest in compelling disclosure, measured by the harm the leak caused, against the public interest in newsgathering, measured by the leaked information's value.[32]

In the case before the court, the leaked information—Plame's CIA affiliation—had little public value, Tatel wrote. But Tatel took a longer view. He worried about the information the public might never learn if the court recognized no common-law privilege at all.[33] The need for an independent judicial evaluation of the damage to newsgathering from enforcing a subpoena was especially important in investigations of leaks that reveal official misconduct or mistakes. The investigators may have improper motives. "Because leak cases typically require the government to investigate itself, if leaks reveal mistakes that high-level officials would have preferred to keep secret, the administration may pursue the source with excessive zeal, regardless of the leaked information's public value."[34]

The question of judicial authority to balance relative harms and how that balance should be conducted also divided the court that, in 2013, enforced the subpoena to the *New York Times* reporter James Risen to testify at the trial of the former CIA agent Jeffrey Sterling. Sterling was charged with giving Risen classified information "about a covert CIA operation pertaining to the Iranian nuclear weapons operation." Risen then used the information in a book. The government wanted Risen to testify at Sterling's trial that Sterling was the source for some of his reporting. A two-judge majority of the federal appeals court in Richmond, Virginia, categorically rejected Risen's claim of a reporter's privilege,[35] both under the First Amendment[36] and under common law.[37] Reporters, in their view, were like everyone else. Judge Gregory, dissenting in part, would have recognized both a constitutional and a common-law privilege. The full appeals court later declined to hear the case.[38]

None of this means that the Court should be asked to revisit *Branzburg* any time soon. There are reasons to do so and reasons to abstain. Among the reasons to do so are the following. *Branzburg* is forty-six years old. The power of institutions, public and private, has grown, as has their capacity to do harm, which increases the importance of investigative reporting. The Court's 4–1, 3–1 division in *Branzburg* makes it a less stable and more ambiguous precedent than the Court has ever acknowledged. Because of its ambiguity, lower court judges are divided on what *Branzburg* actually means. It has been read to say that reporters are no different from any other witness in any kind of case, which would subject them to subpoenas even from private litigants in civil cases. That broad reading is far more consequential to the ability of the press to do its job than if the decision were limited to leak cases, or to grand jury subpoenas (as in *Branzburg* itself), or to criminal cases. *Branzburg* did not address civil cases or criminal-case subpoenas other than from a grand jury because the Court had only a single setting before it.

Perhaps most critical for reporters who investigate wrong-doing by government officials, *Branzburg* was not a leak case. The press might wish to clarify the rule when the crime the government wishes to prosecute is the leak itself. As Judge Tatel wrote, leak investigations deserve added judicial scrutiny because there may be reason to question the motives of government officials in investigating leaks that reveal misconduct or mistakes by other government officials. Nor are all leak cases the same. The subpoenas to Miller and Cooper and the one to Risen illustrate the difference. In Miller's and Cooper's cases, the prosecution lacked proof of the identity of the person who illegally revealed Plame's status to reporters. Or so it claimed. Maybe it just wanted more proof. In Risen's case, the government had ample evidence of the identity of the leaker, whom it was already prosecuting and eventually convicted without Risen's testimony.[39] Should this difference matter? It did matter to Judge Gregory, who dissented in Risen's case. And it could matter to Judges Tatel and Henderson, both of whom said that the government's need was part of the balance.

Another difference between the two cases, which does matter to both Gregory and Tatel, was the public's interest in learning the information leaked to the reporter. The greater the public's interest in the leaked information, the greater the need to protect the identity of the leaker. Judge Tatel concluded, however, that the public's interest in receiving the

information leaked to Miller and Cooper—the CIA affiliation of Valerie Plame—was minimal. By contrast, Judge
Gregory wrote that the "newsworthiness" of the information
leaked to and revealed by Risen "appears to be substantial." It
"portends to inform the reader of a blundered American
intelligence mission in Iran." And, said Gregory, "Risen's
investigation into the methods and capabilities of the United
States foreign intelligence community with respect to the Iranian nuclear program is surely news of the highest import."[40]
Yet several considerations argue against asking the Court to
revisit *Branzburg*. The Court might reach the same result and
then add language that eliminates the ambiguities that have
enabled lower courts to recognize a reporter's privilege when
a subpoena is not from a grand jury. We have what we might
today call anti-*Branzburg* opinions from lower federal courts
that significantly limit *Branzburg's* influence and advance
Press Clause values. A Supreme Court opinion reaffirming
Branzburg might decimate this line of cases.

The Constitution is not the only source of protection against
grand jury and other subpoenas that seek the identity of a
reporter's source or other confidential information. Many
states (but not the federal government) have shield laws that
protect reporters. A state court might rely on the state constitution or, as Judges Tatel and Gregory did, recognize a privilege as a matter of common (or judge-made) law even without
an authorizing statute.

The press can also look to the commitment of self-restraint
memorialized in a Justice Department regulation first adopted
in 1980 and amended several times since, most recently in
2015.[41] Under it, the attorney general must ordinarily approve

subpoenas to the "news media." Subpoenas must be "narrowly drawn" and may be used only

> when the information sought is essential to a successful investigation, prosecution, or litigation; after all reasonable alternative attempts have been made to obtain the information from alternative sources; and after negotiations with the affected member of the news media have been pursued and appropriate notice to the affected member of the news media has been provided.

A shortcoming of this policy is that it is only a policy. It can change tomorrow. And even if it does not change, it does not bind the Justice Department. The "policy is not intended to, and does not, create any right or benefit, substantive or procedural, enforceable at law or in equity."[42] Another problem is that it does not say whom it protects except with the words "news media." Many state shield laws define the protected group in more detail. Does "news media" include documentary filmmakers, scholars, authors of nonfiction books, occasional contributors to a newspaper or magazine, and unaffiliated bloggers? No one in these groups can be confident that it does. Nor can their sources.

Private litigants, meanwhile, are not restrained by the federal government's policies. State prosecutors and state attorneys general are free to set their own policies, subject only to whatever protection state shield laws and court decisions may offer. Some shield laws offer little. In 2006, a federal appellate judge remarked on the diversity of protection in state shield laws. Alaska's statute, for example, at the time required that the person claiming protection be "regularly engaged in the business of collection or writing news for publication or presentation to the public through a news organization." That would exclude casual freelancers and scholars and book authors. Nebraska, by contrast, was at the opposite end of the spectrum. "Nebraska," the judge wrote, "perhaps more in keeping with the spirit of the recent revolutionaries who gave us the First Amendment, [presumably] protects the pamphleteer at the rented printer, and the blogger at the PC, as well as the giant corporation with its New York publishing house."[43]

In 1975, three years after *Branzburg*, Congress adopted Rule 501 of the Federal Rules of Evidence. Its subject is privileges. It allows the federal courts to recognize new privileges "in light of reason and experience," just as they always have. In fact, the Supreme Court used this authority to announce a new privilege for communications between a social worker and a client.[44] It could do the same for a journalist's privilege, as have some lower federal court judges. But it has not shown any inclination to do so, and there is no reason to think that is about to change.

If enacted, the proposed Free Flow of Information Act of 2013, or the less protective alternative of 2017, both described in chapter 2, may be the best we can now do to define the scope of a qualified reporter's privilege in federal cases. And the earlier bill may also be the best way to do it. Perhaps it can be improved, but the balance it strikes seems not only right but also politically necessary. The line drawing here is not easy, whether the line purports to define who is and is not a journalist or the communications the privilege does and does not protect. These are issues that legislation can resolve more effectively than can courts through piecemeal litigation. An absolute privilege, one that credits no other interest as superior to the interest of a journalist in protecting a source's identity, is wrong as a matter of public policy and also strategy. Other interests in the Free Flow of Information Act—for example, when necessary to prevent a kidnapping—may rightly outweigh the reporter's wish to conceal a source's identity.[45] Nor are the law's narrow exceptions likely to deter sources. Claiming that other interests are always subordinate to the press interest—which is what an absolute privilege means—would be a strategic error, a sure way to lose public support. Privileges for communications with others—lawyers, doctors, clergy, and spouses—have exceptions germane to the particular relationship. Journalists should not claim to be more important.

5

PRESS CLAUSE PROTECTION FOR NEWSGATHERING

I n addition to protection against liability for defamation and privacy invasion and the right to protect confidential sources without risking jail, the press needs protection for how it gathers news. This includes access to places closed to the public, like prisons and jails, unless good reasons justify exclusion. In rare circumstances, the press should also be able to enter the private property of nongovernmental actors. In *Branzburg v. Hayes*, the Supreme Court wrote, "news gathering is not without its First Amendment protections."[1] Although six years later it tried to walk back that statement as a superfluous remark without any precedential value,[2] lower courts have treated it seriously.

Journalists should not get a passkey to go wherever they wish and to do whatever they want for the sake of a story. There are limits. The challenge is to define them. But the limits cannot be described with precision. How, then, can a journalist or an editor know what is allowed and what is not? When access is negotiated—to inspect prisons or enter war zones, for example—there is clarity. So, too, if courts find a right of access, as they have for courtrooms.[3] But where access relies on deception or is surreptitious, there is uncertainty. The press takes a chance. Eventually, a court will decide whether press freedom justified the conduct. As courts decide more of those cases, a body of law will have emerged that makes prediction easier. This is not ideal, but it is no different from the risk of liability for defamation or privacy invasion, where constitutional protection is strong but not absolute.

A key distinction is needed. Let's say the press lawfully acquires and then publishes information about a person. She may sue, claiming that although the press did nothing illegal to learn the information, disclosing it violated her right to keep the information private. Some states do recognize a claim based on public disclosure of private facts even if those facts were learned through lawful means and are true. It is also possible, however, that to get the information a journalist will have acted unlawfully. For example, a journalist may trespass on private property, invade a person's privacy by secretly recording a conversation or conduct, or engage in an act of deception that the law forbids. Then, the plaintiff may make two claims: One for the publication and another for how the information in it was acquired. The distinction is between *what* the press discloses, which a plaintiff may claim violates her rights, and *how* the press acquires the information it discloses, which the plaintiff may allege constitutes a separate violation of her rights.

The argument in this chapter will likely be the most controversial in the book because to facilitate newsgathering, it proposes to give members of the press a right that no one outside law enforcement has. It subordinates some property and privacy rights to the press's (and therefore the public's) interest in newsgathering. But the proposal here is not entirely revolutionary. As we will see, some subordination occurs even today, depending on the particular rights being subordinated. While these rights are described in various ways among American jurisdictions, they are all aimed at the same thing— the protection of property, privacy, or solitude. Three legal doctrines are especially prominent.

TRESPASS

The Restatement of the Law of Torts, a highly influential document from the private but nonprofit American Law Institute, defines trespass this way: "One is subject to liability to another for trespass, irrespective of whether he thereby causes harm to any legally protected interest of the other, if he intentionally . . . enters land in the possession of the other."[4] Consent to trespass allows entry but not if the consent is "induced" by "misrepresentation." All that is required to commit trespass is the intention to commit it. The absence of harm does not matter, although it may mean that the property owner has no or only nominal damages and will not sue and that a prosecutor will not prosecute. Think of someone who takes a shortcut across an open field.

Building on trespass laws, states have passed laws to prevent animal rights and environmental groups, the press, and others from filming or photographing on land, either through surreptitious entry or by misrepresenting themselves to gain access, in order to publicize the harsh treatment of animals or harm to the environment. These laws have been called "ag-gag" laws. They prevent discovery of information in which the public may have a strong interest and which may also be criminal.

INTRUSION

In addition to the law of trespass, two other kinds of actionable conduct may frustrate newsgathering. First is the prohibition against intrusion, which is meant to protect privacy. Although it overlaps trespass, intrusion is a distinct legal concept. The Restatement of Torts defines intrusion this way: "One who intentionally intrudes, physically or otherwise, upon the solitude or seclusion of another or his private affairs or concerns, is subject to liability to the other for invasion of his privacy, if the intrusion would be highly offensive to a reasonable person."[5] Intrusion short of trespass would include, for example, taking photographs of someone in their backyard using a telephoto lens. This language does not recognize a defense based on newsgathering unless a court were to construe the words "highly offensive" to allow proof that the information gained by intrusion is of such concern to the public that the intrusion should not be deemed highly offensive. The more newsworthy the information, the greater may be a court's tolerance for the intrusion, depending, of course, on the nature of the intrusion. So taking a picture of two politicians talking on a park bench might not be highly offensive, but planting a listening device on the underside of the bench could be. They must expect to be photographed but not eavesdropped on with hidden technology.

DISCLOSURE OF PRIVATE FACTS

Last is the tort of public disclosure of private facts, which the Restatement of Torts labels "Publicity Given to Private Life" and defines this way:

> One who gives publicity to a matter concerning the private life of another is subject to liability to the other for invasion of his privacy, if the matter publicized is of a kind that
>
> (a) would be highly offensive to a reasonable person, and
>
> (b) is not of legitimate concern to the public.[6]

The press might acquire private facts without trespass or intrusion (or any other unlawful conduct). Then the only question is whether it is free to report those facts. The Restatement says it is, even if the disclosure "would be highly offensive to a reasonable person," if the information is about a matter "of legitimate concern to the public." This is a clear recognition of the importance of the press. While the protection it offers is available to anyone, including local gossips, as a practical matter it will be the press that most often takes advantage of it because the words "public" and "publicity" imply that the information has been disclosed by publishing or broadcasting.

Should the press also be permitted to engage in trespass or intrusion if the information sought concerns a matter of "legitimate concern to the public?" Adding such an exception would be a conceptual leap. Now we are no longer talking about publication of "private facts" that the press has lawfully discovered or received but about discovering those facts through conduct that would be unlawful if performed by others. In considering whether to make this leap, we must answer two questions. First, when if ever would the interest in newsgathering (and in reporting a matter of public concern) justify trespass or intrusion? Second, if we do create a newsgathering exception to laws forbidding trespass and intrusion, who will decide if the exception applies? The issue of who decides arises even today when the press discloses private facts lawfully acquired (i.e., without trespass or intrusion). How do we answer it? Will the answer be the same where the conduct is not merely disclosure of private facts but trespass or intrusion to gather the facts? These are difficult questions that require us to recognize the legitimate property and privacy interests of others as well as the interest in newsgathering and the public interest.

THE *FOOD LION* CASE

The 1999 *Food Lion* decision from the Fourth Circuit Court of Appeals in Richmond, Virginia, is a good place to begin the search for answers.[7] The facts are echoed, with variations, in other media cases before and since. ABC had been told that "Food Lion stores were engaging in unsanitary meat-handling practices," including a charge that "employees ground out-of-date beef together with new beef, bleached rank meat to remove its odor, and re-dated (and offered for sale) products not sold before their printed expiration date." Producers at the ABC show *PrimeTime Live* "decided to conduct an undercover investigation of Food Lion." Two reporters, Lynne Dale and Susan Barnett, applied for jobs there. Their applications had "false identities and references and fictitious local addresses." They concealed their current employment with ABC and "otherwise misrepresented their educational and employment experiences." Barnett was hired as a deli clerk in South Carolina. Dale got a job as a trainee meat wrapper in North Carolina. Barnett stayed two weeks, Dale one week. "As they went about their assigned tasks for Food

Lion, Dale and Barnett used tiny cameras ('lipstick' cameras, for example) and microphones concealed on their bodies to secretly record Food Lion employees."[8]
The recordings revealed dramatic scenes tending to show that Food Lion mishandled and mislabeled food.

> The broadcast included, for example, videotape that appeared to show Food Lion employees repackaging and redating fish that had passed the expiration date, grinding expired beef with fresh beef, and applying barbeque sauce to chicken past its expiration date in order to mask the smell and sell it as fresh in the gourmet food section. . . . The truth of the *PrimeTime Live* broadcast was not an issue in the litigation we now describe.

Food Lion sued ABC and the *PrimeTime Live* producers and reporters. Food Lion's suit focused *not* on the broadcast, as a defamation suit would, but on the methods ABC used to obtain the video footage. The grocery chain asserted claims of fraud, breach of the duty of loyalty, trespass, and unfair trade practices, seeking millions in compensatory damages.[9]

ABC's conduct presents a classic example of one strategy useful to investigative reporters. We have deception that enabled reporters to enter a private space (here a physical space), surreptitious electronic recording in the space, and broadcast of the recorded events. We will see the same pattern with some variation in other cases. The jury found the ABC reporters (and therefore ABC as their employer) guilty of disloyalty, trespass, and, because the reporters had lied about their long-range employment intentions, fraud. It awarded Food Lion $1,402 in compensatory damages, $1,400 of which was based on the finding of fraud, and then added five million dollars in punitive damages as punishment for the fraud. The trial judge reduced the punitive damages to $315,000.

The court of appeals overturned the finding of fraud. Notwithstanding what Food Lion may have assumed, "Dale and Barnett did not make any express representations about how long they would work."[10] That ruling automatically eliminated the punitive damages, which depended on the finding of fraud, and all but two dollars of the compensatory award. But the court upheld the finding that the reporters violated their duty of loyalty to Food Lion—they were *really* loyal to ABC—and the finding of trespass. The trespass occurred when Dale and Barnett entered nonpublic areas of the store and secretly filmed. However, Food Lion had sought only "nominal" damages for disloyalty and trespass, probably because it could not prove that *by themselves* (apart from the ensuing broadcast) the trespass and disloyalty caused it any harm at all.

I emphasize "by themselves" because Food Lion also argued that the trespass and disloyalty, even if causing only nominal damages, nevertheless led to the broadcast, which caused substantial damages through loss of "good will" and "sales." The trial judge, however, rejected damages for loss of good will and sales. He said that those losses "were the direct result of diminished consumer confidence in the store."[11] The trespass made the story possible, true, but the trespass did not cause the lost business. Food Lion's practices did. Food Lion would therefore get no damages based on the broadcast. The appeals court agreed that Food Lion could not get damages for lost business and good will as a result of the broadcast (sometimes called *publication damages*), but it had a different reason. We are now getting into some rather fine distinctions, but they are distinctions with profound consequences for investigative reporting.

The appeals court's explanation for rejecting publication damages returns us to 1964 and the landmark case *New York Times v. Sullivan*. Recall that *New York Times* held that a public official (later extended to include public figures) could not get damages under state defamation claims unless a reporter acted with actual malice, which the Court defined to mean knowledge that the allegedly defamatory statement was false or made with reckless disregard for whether it was true or false.[12] Food Lion did not sue for defamation, because it could not prove actual malice and falsity. The broadcast was true, and a true statement cannot be defamatory. "What Food Lion sought to do" instead, the appeals court wrote, "was to recover defamation-type damages under non-reputational tort claims, without satisfying the stricter (First Amendment) standards of a defamation claim."[13] Translation: Damages from the broadcast would have required Food Lion to prove both falsity and actual malice *if* it had elected to sue for defamation, which it could not do. Food Lion could not avoid these two *New York Times* requirements simply by changing its theory of liability from defamation to something else—that is, disloyalty and trespass. And the reason it could not do "such an end-run around First Amendment strictures"[14] is explained by two other important Supreme Court decisions from the post–*New York Times* era. The media lost one of those cases and won the other.

PUBLICATION DAMAGES:
HUSTLER AND *COHEN*

In 1983, using the style of a Campari advertisement, *Hustler* magazine published a parody that portrayed the Reverend Jerry Falwell, founder of the "Moral Majority."[15] Where actual Campari ads describe the "first time" someone has tried Campari (while taking advantage of the sexual innuendo), the *Hustler* parody implied that Falwell's first sexual encounter was with his mother.[16] Falwell sued *Hustler* for libel and for intentional infliction of emotional distress. The jury rejected Falwell's libel claim because no one could possibly have believed the parody to be "describing actual facts about [Falwell]."[17] But it upheld the emotional-distress claim and awarded Falwell $150,000.

In 1988, in an opinion by Chief Justice Rehnquist, the Supreme Court overturned the verdict for Falwell. Even though his claim was one for intentional infliction of emotional distress, not defamation, the First Amendment required Falwell to satisfy the *New York Times* actual-malice standard anyway.[18] True, the *Hustler* parody implied a false fact—that Falwell and his mother were sexually intimate—and we can be certain that editors knew it was false; nonetheless, the "fact" was not deemed false in the eyes of the law, because no one would believe it, which is why the jury rejected the libel claim. That left the emotional-distress claim. The Court said that Falwell had to prove actual malice anyway, and he could not. Even if *Hustler* was motivated by "hatred or ill-will," the First Amendment protected such motives "in the area of public debate about public figures."[19] In other words, *Hustler* was not guilty of the kind of malice that the *New York Times* case requires.

The *Food Lion* court followed this reasoning. Food Lion's effort to get reputational damages from the broadcast, based on trespass and disloyalty claims was, like Falwell's emotional-harm claim, foreclosed by the requirement that it prove actual malice, which it could not. ABC's motive was not malicious. Its motive was to expose the sale of adulterated foods. The importance of this ruling to the press is hard to overstate. From ABC's and its reporters' perspective, while a finding of trespass and disloyalty may be regrettable, if damages are only two dollars it may conclude that the story was worth it. Indeed, a future Food Lion is unlikely even to sue, given the cost of doing so, to achieve so nominal a victory.

Or maybe the damages won't be nominal after all. The *Food Lion* court had to choose between the analysis in *Hustler* and the analysis in another Supreme Court case, *Cohen v. Cowles Media Company*, decided in 1991.[20] The *Food Lion* court followed *Hustler*, but another federal court might follow *Cohen*. Editors and media lawyers weighing a decision whether to publish will have to predict which of these decisions applies. This will not be easy, because they are hard to reconcile.

Dan Cohen sued Cowles Media after reporters for the *Minneapolis Star Tribune* broke a promise not to reveal his identity. Relying on that promise, Cohen, who was associated with Wheelock Whitney's 1982 gubernatorial campaign in Minnesota, gave the paper copies of two public records. They allegedly disclosed that an opposing candidate had once been charged with unlawful assembly and had been convicted of petit theft. The ensuing story identified Cohen as the paper's source, in violation of the promise, and Cohen's employer fired him. He sued, and a jury awarded him $200,000. The state supreme court held that disclosure of Cohen's identity violated the state's law of promissory estoppel, which essentially means that Cowles made a promise, Cohen relied on the promise by doing something (becoming a source) he would not otherwise have done, and then Cowles broke its promise, which ended Cohen's job. But the state supreme court reversed Cohen's victory anyway because, it said, the First Amendment gave Cowles a defense to liability under state law. The state court balanced Cohen's interest in anonymity against the newsworthiness of the fact that Cohen was the source, and Cohen lost. It was in the public's interest to know that a person working on candidate Whitney's campaign was leaking negative information about an opponent, even if disclosure of Cohen as the leaker required the newspaper to break a promise.[21]

The Supreme Court reversed. It posed two questions. The first question was whether the First Amendment did in fact prevent enforcement of Minnesota's promissory estoppel law, as the Minnesota court believed.[22] The Supreme Court said it did not. It invoked a "well-established line of decisions holding that generally applicable laws do not offend the First Amendment simply because their enforcement against the press has incidental effects on the ability to gather and report the news."[23] This doctrine—that the press is not exempt from laws of general application despite the effect on newsgathering—also explains the absence of a newsgathering exception to laws forbidding trespass, intrusion, employee disloyalty, and other laws. The press does not get immunity from laws that apply to everyone, although, as I will argue, it sometimes should.

Of immediate interest to us, in light of *Food Lion*, is the second question before the Court in *Cohen*. Cowles Media argued that even if, despite the First Amendment, Cohen had a claim against it based on the law of promissory estoppel, his damages could not include any harm he suffered (like job loss) because it published his name. What Cowles published was true, it argued, and the press could not be held liable for publishing the truth, even if it broke a promise in doing so. Perhaps Cohen would be entitled to damages for the broken promise, but that would get him nowhere. The broken promise by itself caused no damage. Cowles relied on *Hustler*, which denied Falwell emotional-distress damages for the publication of the mock Campari advertisement because a parody of a public figure, even one as tasteless as the mock advertisement, was not actual malice. Cohen also had to prove actual malice, Cowles argued, and could not.

Although the *Hustler* decision persuaded the *Food Lion* court to deny the store damages from ABC's broadcast, it did not persuade the Supreme Court to deny Cohen damages for the *Star Tribune*'s publication. The Court dismissively wrote:

> Nor is Cohen attempting to use a promissory estoppel cause of action to avoid the strict requirements for establishing a libel or defamation claim. . . . Cohen is not seeking damages for injury to his reputation or his state of mind. He sought damages . . . for a breach of a promise that caused him to lose his job and lowered his earning capacity. Thus, this is not a case like [*Hustler*], where we held that the constitutional libel standards apply to a claim alleging that the publication of a parody was a state law tort of intentional infliction of emotional distress.[24]

In other words, Cohen's lost income was not *New York Times*–type (i.e., reputational) damages, whereas the emotional harm that Falwell allegedly suffered was. So Cohen did not have to prove actual malice, while Falwell did. This attempt to differentiate the two cases may sound like the law, or at least the Supreme Court, has gone down Alice's rabbit hole. Justice Blackmun (joined by Justices Marshall and Souter) thought so. He would have recognized Cowles' First Amendment defense. He wrote:

The majority attempts to distinguish *Hustler* on the ground that there the plaintiff sought damages for injury to his state of mind whereas the petitioner here sought damages "for a breach of a promise that caused him to lose his job and lowered his earning capacity." I perceive no meaningful distinction between a statute that penalizes published speech in order to protect the individual's psychological well being or reputational interest and one that exacts the same penalty in order to compensate the loss of employment or earning potential. Certainly, our decision in *Hustler* recognized no such distinction.[25]

Lower courts must try to make sense of the Supreme Court's fine distinctions, which can sometimes be a challenge. The *Food Lion* court struggled to reconcile *Cohen* and *Hustler*. Which case was Food Lion's claim more like? *Food Lion* chose *Hustler*. Like Falwell, the store sought damages for reputational harm from publication (or broadcast) and therefore had to prove actual malice under *New York Times*. Cohen, by contrast, did not seek damages for reputational harm but rather, as the Supreme Court described it, "for breach of a promise that caused him to lose his job and lowered his earning capacity," so he did not have to prove actual malice. Of course, his lower earning capacity will result, at least in part, from the harm to his reputation, but let that go. The issues here are only nominally about law anyway. They are really about public policy.

Justice Souter's separate dissent in *Cohen* (joined by Justices Marshall, Blackmun, and O'Connor) and Justice Breyer's concurrence (joined by Justice O'Connor) in a case a decade later challenge the view that the press is never exempt from laws of general applicability. The press *should*, at times, be exempt from such laws, Souter argued, so that it can discover and report information to the public. The information that Cohen was the leaker presented just such a time. To appreciate Souter's and Breyer's different views and their consequences to freedom of the press, it is first necessary to take a step back.

A NEWSWORTHINESS EXCEPTION TO GENERALLY APPLICABLE LAWS

How Would It Work?

In *Food Lion*, we have a model for cases in which subjects of an investigative story seek compensation, either for the conduct that enabled the reporter to learn the information, for the harm caused by the publication of that information, or for both. (Usually both, because if you're going to sue, you might as well sue on all plausible claims and for all damages possibly available.) Variations from this model are several.

First, the *theory of liability* may vary. In *Food Lion*, the court found trespass and disloyalty. But if a reporter does not enter a physical space that belongs to another, trespass is unavailable. If she did not get her story by impersonating a job applicant while working for someone else, a disloyalty claim is unavailable. But trespass and disloyalty do not exhaust the available reasons for liability. Others are intrusion, invasion of privacy, deception, and unlawful recording. These may be combined. Liability in these cases is usually governed by state law. For investigative reporting, the critical question is: When will the First Amendment block liability under these state laws even though they are laws that purportedly apply to everyone?

Second, the *space or interest invaded* may vary. In a California case, a television station reporting on responses to highway accidents intruded on a conversation between medical personnel and a woman pinned under a car. The station wired a nurse who was treating the woman. After transfer to a helicopter ambulance, it recorded the woman's voice and image in the helicopter. The California Supreme Court ruled that this conduct would constitute intrusion if, on remand, the jury concluded that it was "highly offensive" unless it was "justified by the legitimate motive of gathering the news."[26] In yet another case, a television reporter, misrepresenting her credentials, got a job at a company that offered "telepsychic" readings to customers who called a 900 telephone number (and were charged by the minute for the duration of the call). The reporter secretly audio and video recorded her conversations with other telepsychics, including Mark Sanders. She then included excerpts of the recordings in a broadcast about the telepsychic industry. The California Supreme Court wrote that although Sanders had no expectation of privacy in his conversations, which other employees could overhear and which the reporter was free to repeat, he did have a reasonable expectation that the conversations would not be recorded. But as before, the court wrote that a newsgathering motive might offer a defense.[27]

Into this stew we must add one other highly consequential Supreme Court opinion. In *Bartnicki v. Vopper*, two union officials sued a radio station and others.[28] The station had broadcast a surreptitious recording of a telephone call between the union officials. The person who made the recording was not known. The tape made its way to the station, which had done nothing unlawful to get it. The union officials' conversation was newsworthy for two reasons: Its subject was a local labor dispute between teachers and the school board, and it was susceptible to the inference that the officials contemplated violence.

The person who recorded the conversation committed a federal crime. It was also a crime for the station to broadcast the recording if it knew that it was recorded illegally. No one was prosecuted, but the union officials sued the station for damages, which federal statutes also allowed. The question for the Court was "both novel and narrow,"[29] Justice Stevens wrote in 2001. Did the First Amendment give the radio station a constitutional defense to civil liability even if it knew that the recording was illegally obtained? The station argued that it did because the broadcast was newsworthy. The majority agreed. Here we see a holding that some courts have been reluctant to reach when the basis for liability is intrusion or trespass. A person who violates a federal criminal law may be immune to civil liability, and even criminal liability, because the First Amendment will protect public disclosure of newsworthy information.[30]

But not always. The press does not get carte blanche to ignore laws that apply to everyone. Nor can the press be the final arbiter of whether in a particular instance newsgathering will justify conduct that would otherwise be unlawful. The answer will depend on criteria we can broadly describe, but the courts get the final word, as they do now in all First Amendment cases, including those alleging defamation and invasion of privacy. The *Bartnicki* Court had to rely on the First Amendment to circumvent congressional statutes because the statutes did not recognize a newsworthiness defense. But courts, not Congress or state lawmakers, create common law through their decisions and are free to modify it without having to rely on the Constitution.

A newsworthiness exception to laws that apply to everyone can build on the analysis in Justice Breyer's concurring opinion in *Bartnicki* and the more significant analysis in Justice Souter's dissent in *Cohen v. Cowles Media*, where reporters broke a promise not to identify a source.

In recognizing First Amendment immunity for the radio station in *Bartnicki*, Justice Breyer, joined by Justice O'Connor, expanded on Justice Stevens's opinion for the Court. He stressed that the tape "involved a matter of unusual public concern."[31] He then went on to use language especially germane to the argument here.

> I would ask whether the statutes strike a reasonable balance between their speech-restricting and speech-enhancing consequences. Or do they instead impose restrictions on speech that are disproportionate when measured against their corresponding privacy and speech-related benefits, taking into account the kind, the importance, and the extent of these benefits, as well as the need for the restrictions in order to secure those benefits? What this Court has called "strict scrutiny"—with its strong presumption against constitutionality—is normally out of place where, as here, important competing constitutional interests are implicated.[32]

For Breyer, it was necessary that the Court "balance" two interests—the interest in privacy in the recorded calls and the interest in disclosure of truthful information of public importance. He said that the statutes before the Court

> ensure the privacy of telephone conversations much as a trespass statute ensures privacy within the home. That assurance of privacy helps to overcome our natural

reluctance to discuss private matters when we fear that our private conversations may become public. And the statutory restrictions consequently encourage conversations that otherwise might not take place.[33]

Furthermore, he wrote, categorically exempting "media" from the prohibition against further dissemination of private conversations will often "cause the speakers serious harm over and above the harm caused by an initial disclosure to the person who intercepted the phone call." The plaintiffs had a legitimate argument that the statute should apply full force to the radio station because the broadcast multiplied the harm to their privacy. If, instead, the First Amendment allowed the media to escape liability whenever it was the passive recipient of an illegal recording, the aims of the statute—to protect the privacy of telephone conversations—would be seriously undermined.

Yet Breyer ruled in favor of the radio station anyway because there were considerations on the other side of the ledger that were weightier than the privacy interests of the union officials. "As applied in these circumstances," Breyer wrote, the statutes "do not reasonably reconcile the competing constitutional objectives. Rather, they disproportionately interfere with media freedom." In reaching this conclusion, Breyer stressed, first, that the radio station did nothing unlawful to get the tapes. Second, the plaintiffs were "'limited public figures,' for they voluntarily engaged in a public controversy. They thereby subjected themselves to somewhat greater public scrutiny and had a lesser interest in privacy than an individual engaged in purely private affairs." Third, "the speakers had little or no *legitimate* interest in maintaining the privacy of the particular conversation" because the conversation suggested "threats to public safety."[34] Although "the danger may

have passed by the time of publication, that fact cannot legit-
imize the speaker's earlier privacy expectation. Nor should
editors, who must make a publication decision quickly, have
to determine present or continued danger before publishing
this kind of threat."[35] When it was all added up, the union
officials' "legitimate privacy expectations are unusually low,
and the public interest in defeating those expectations is
unusually high."[36]

In Breyer's concurrence we can identify factors that a
court should weigh in deciding whether media conduct that
invades a legally protected space should nevertheless be protected because of the truthful information the invasion provides and its value to the public. In listing those factors, we
should especially take note that Breyer refers to "the media"
and the need of "editors" to make decisions under time constraints. Justice Stevens's majority opinion did not explicitly
do that, perhaps because the Court remains wedded to the
desire to avoid giving the Press Clause any content that is not
already present in the Speech Clause and available to everyone. The Court could hardly maintain that pretense if it
began to cite the special role of the media in disclosing matters of public interest and the responsibility of editors to
weigh that interest against private interests.

Balancing the competing interests was also endorsed in
Justice Souter's 1991 dissent for himself and three others
(Justices Marshall, Blackmun, and O'Connor) in *Cohen*, the
broken-promise case. Souter rejected the argument, which
the majority accepted, that there is no role for the First
Amendment to play when liability is imposed under a law
applicable to everyone. Souter also rejected the argument
that Cowles Media had only itself to blame for the restriction on its right to publish. True, its reporters had made the

promise not to disclose Cohen's identity, "but freedom of the press is ultimately founded on the value of enhancing such discourse for the sake of a citizenry better informed and thus more prudently self-governed." Souter then explained why in this case the "balance" favored the First Amendment interest:

> There can be no doubt that the fact of Cohen's identity expanded the universe of information relevant to the choice faced by Minnesota voters in that State's 1982 gubernatorial election. . . . The propriety of his leak to respondents could be taken to reflect on his character, which in turn could be taken to reflect on the character of the candidate who had retained him as an adviser.

Souter went on to say that on different facts the balance could tilt against the press. In each case, the Court should consider the importance of the information and how the press got it.

> One can conceive of situations in which the injured party is a private individual, whose identity is of less public concern than that of [Cohen]; liability there might not be constitutionally prohibited. Nor do I mean to imply that the circumstances of acquisition are irrelevant to the balance, although they may go only to what balances against, and not to diminish, the First Amendment value of any particular piece of information.[37]

Building on Breyer's and Souter's criteria for balancing privacy interests against First Amendment values, we can begin to fill in some more blanks in deciding when the press will be exempt from a law that applies to everyone else. We can begin to describe when claims like intrusion, trespass, eavesdropping, and misrepresentation should give way to press interests—or more precisely, as Souter recognized, to the interests of "a citizenry better informed and thus more prudently self-governed."[38] The press serves the public. Ultimately, judges will make this decision as a matter of constitutional or common-law interpretation, but clarity will assist editorial judgments.

Factors for deciding whether the Press Clause should immunize conduct that would otherwise be a basis for liability under laws of general applicability include, first, whether the particular newsgathering activity was the product of editorial judgment that weighed the nature of the intrusion (or trespass or other tort) against the importance to the public of the information it was intended to uncover. Did someone perform that task in light of journalistic values? In an extended investigation, we would expect ongoing editorial oversight. Editorial judgment is cited in media-law litigation as part of what makes the press the press. Editorial decisions do not, of course, bind the courts, but when they reflect deliberation (within the time constraints the story imposes) and are informed by First Amendment values, judges have deferred. This deference is most obvious in cases rejecting challenges to the publication of true information on the ground that the publication disclosed private facts. In reviewing the editorial judgment in cases of trespass and intrusion, courts should similarly evaluate the seriousness of any interference with a plaintiff's privacy interests. Breaking into an office or unlawfully recording a phone call will always be unacceptable. Not so would be walking across an unenclosed field or applying for a job using a false résumé (as in *Food Lion*). (In *Bartnicki*, the radio station was the innocent recipient of the intercepted call.) In this mix also goes consideration of the actual harm from the privacy invasion itself. Crossing an open field will usually cause no harm. Courts should independently evaluate, as Justices Souter and Breyer did, the public interest in the information. Revealing that a supermarket regularly sells adulterated food would rank high on the public-interest scale, as would dangers to public health generally or corruption in government. Revelations about a celebrity's love affairs would not rank as high, notwithstanding public curiosity. Likewise, the public's interest in learning that a "telepsychic" enterprise is a sham is by comparison low. But it would be stronger for an investigation that uncovers fake insurance claims or shoddy practices in a medical clinic.[39] The identity of the target of a media investigation matters, too, as it did in *Bartnicki*, where the overheard telephone calls were between union officials, not regular union members. This factor comports with the *New York Times* line of cases, which cites the public nature of the plaintiff (public official or public figure) as a justification for constitutional protection from liability for defamation claims. Yet another consideration is the availability of other investigative tools. Did the press try to get the information in less intrusive ways? Was the privacy invasion proportionate to the needs of the story?[40]

Consider this hypothetical investigation. The statehouse reporter for a newspaper gets unconfirmed and not-for-attribution information that the speaker of the state assembly is doing official favors for those who refer clients to his daughter's law firm. The conduct alleged would violate state ethics rules and is likely a crime. Weeks of effort to confirm the information prove unavailing. In order to learn more, and because the information the paper has received is detailed and credible, editors send a young reporter, using a fake résumé, to secure a job as a summer intern in the speaker's office. One of her jobs is to answer the phone. Another is to open and print emails. She keeps a record of the identities of all callers and visitors. She makes copies of select items from the emails she is authorized to download. Editors (perhaps advised by a media lawyer) monitor her activity. The information she discovers enables the newspaper to investigate further and then to report that the speaker has indeed advanced legislation and done favors for individuals or companies that have sent business to his daughter's law firm. The speaker is forced to give up his leadership position and loses his seat in the next election. The US attorney begins an investigation.

The newspaper's efforts may violate laws against intrusion, trespass, and disloyalty. Should its motive—to expose the wrongdoing of a public official—give it a defense to civil liability when the speaker sues? Should the paper be liable for publication damages—that is, the ensuing loss of the speaker's post and then his seat—as well as whatever damages flow from the intrusion or trespass itself, which are likely to be nominal, as they were in *Food Lion?* I answer the first question yes and the second no. The newsworthiness of the information should defeat a civil action for intrusion, trespass, or disloyalty. And if it did not defeat a liability claim, then the newspaper should not be liable for damages from publication of the truthful information but only for the harm, if any, that flowed directly from the reporter's subterfuge.[41]

Today, many courts analyzing my hypothetical would ask whether the reporter committed trespass because she gained access to a nonpublic place, a portion of the speaker's office, by deception, thereby vitiating the consent to enter. They would also consider whether by keeping a record of phone calls and making copies of emails she violated some other duty to the speaker, perhaps a duty of loyalty. In addressing liability for trespass and disloyalty, these courts would not consider the fact that the reporter was a reporter. Because the Press Clause and press status would be ignored, the case would be decided the same way whatever the actor's status. Yet even courts whose analysis proceeds that way might feel a need to recognize the press interest without actually saying so. To accommodate the press (and therefore the public) interest, the court might be tempted to say that the reporter did nothing unlawful. The court does not then have to balance the press and public interest against the interests protected by the law that the reporter may have violated. Everyone would be able to act the same way. Refusal to recognize the press interest, in other words, encourages the courts to interpret the law to accommodate the press interest without acknowledging it, but at the price of weakening the law's privacy objectives. More likely, a court would not choose this path. More likely it would uphold the plaintiff's claim and treat the reporter's status as legally irrelevant. Whether it would reject damages flowing from the publication, as in *Hustler* and *Food Lion*, or allow them, as in *Cohen*, is harder to predict.

Desnick v. American Broadcasting Companies, Inc. is a good example of what a court might do to avoid giving the press rights unavailable to others. In March 1993, journalists with concealed cameras and posing as patients requested eye examinations at Desnick's clinics, which performed thousands of cataract operations yearly for which they billed Medicare. The ensuing program on *PrimeTime Live* reported that Medicare was billed for operations that were medically unnecessary. The company that owned the clinics sued for trespass and other claims. Judge Posner, taking the conventional view, wrote that "there is no journalists' privilege to trespass."[42] ABC argued that there was no trespass because the reporters had consent to enter the clinics. The clinics replied that the consent was no good because it had been procured through fraud. The reporters had misrepresented themselves. Posner cited cases in which fraud both did and did not vitiate consent to enter private property. The fraud here did not. Why not? "The test patients entered offices that were open to anyone expressing a desire for ophthalmic services and videotaped physicians engaged in professional, not personal, communications with strangers (the testers themselves). The activities of the offices were not disrupted. Nor was there any 'invasion of a person's private space.'"[43]

If Posner had recognized a newsgathering defense to a trespass claim, he could have cited the very same facts to hold that the defense applied. One might ask what difference it makes. The case would be decided the same way. Perhaps there would have been no difference in *Desnick*, but in similar cases the same court (or on the very same facts a different court) might conclude that the clinics' privacy claim prevailed. Without a defense for newsgathering, ABC would have lost. Similarly, in my hypothetical about the assembly speaker, a court might find an unlawful trespass into the speaker's office because the reporter misrepresented her purpose. A court might also find that the speaker's privacy rights were violated when the reporter kept copies of emails, possibly even when she read them. Then, in order to avoid a verdict for the speaker, a court would have to say that there *is* a journalist's privilege to trespass. Not an unlimited privilege. It would depend on the nature of the intrusion and the public interest in the information learned.

Some courts do seem willing to recognize a "journalist's exception." An academic psychologist wrote an article about the reliability of adult memories of childhood sexual abuse. A woman anonymously named in the article (as "Jane Doe") claimed that the researcher had misrepresented her status in order to persuade Doe's foster mother to disclose Doe's personal information. The lawsuit seems to have alarmed news organizations: many of them filed an amicus brief defending the use of deception in newsgathering. They argued "that permitting a subject about whom unflattering information has been obtained from a third party source to sue the reporter or investigator for offensive intrusion into the subject's privacy . . . would have an undesirable chilling effect on the gathering and publication of newsworthy material." The court held that the particular misrepresentation in the case before it might have crossed a line because of the highly personal information the researcher wanted. Whether it did so would be decided at trial. But the court also recognized "the danger and inadvisability of adopting a broad rule under which any type of misrepresentation by a reporter, investigator, or scholar to obtain information would be considered sufficient to support a cause of action for intrusion into private matters."⁴⁴

A newspaper deciding whether to employ subterfuge takes a risk even with Press Clause protection. A court might decide that the public's interest in the story did not justify the tactics used to get it. The same risk is present today if the press is charged with invasion of privacy by disclosing private facts *lawfully* obtained. A court today might decide that the disclosed facts, though true and lawfully obtained, are highly offensive to a reasonable person and not of legitimate concern to the public. In making this "legitimate concern" assessment in claims of privacy invasion, courts defer to, but are not bound by, editorial judgment. They prefer not to make the newsworthiness decision, but neither do they abdicate their responsibility to review it. The same should be true where the facts are secured through intrusion, trespass, electronic eavesdropping, deception, or the like.

The nature of the conduct is important. Burglary is not justified. Hacking into a computer network or a voicemail system is unacceptable.[45] Press interests will not always justify uninvited entry into a business establishment that is otherwise open to the public. They were not when, during lunch, a CBS reporter and a camera crew disrupted a Manhattan restaurant that had been cited for health-code violations.[46] But general prohibitions against trespass, deception, disloyalty, and conflict of interest may at times have to yield after weighing the public interest in the information against the need for and nature of the particular investigative method. Courts must balance the interests a law protects against the interest in disclosure. Privacy should not always win.

AG-GAG LAWS

Ag-gag laws provide a good example of how judicial balancing might inform the Press Clause. These laws forbid trespass on private land when the trespasser's purpose is, for example, to document mistreatment of animals or environmental dangers. As such, they are what we might call "trespass plus" laws. Ag-gag laws in Idaho and Wyoming have been challenged in federal court with mixed results. Although these challenges do not test the reach of the Press Clause, because the plaintiffs, who were mostly not from the legacy press,[47] relied instead on the First Amendment's Speech and

Petition Clauses and the Fourteenth Amendment's Equal Protection Clause, the reasoning of the courts in each case can be used in defining the reach of the Press Clause. In fact, the Ninth Circuit Court of Appeals in San Francisco, addressing the Idaho law, explicitly recognized the relevance of its decision for investigative reporting.

After an animal-rights group in Idaho "released a video of workers using a moving tractor to drag a cow on the floor by a chain attached to her neck and workers repeatedly beating, kicking and jumping on cows," the Idaho Dairymen's Association lobbied successfully for a law defining the crime of "interference with agricultural production."[48] Among other things, the law prohibits getting a job in or gaining entry to "an agricultural production facility" by "misrepresentation." It also prohibits entering a facility without permission and making "audio or video recordings of the conduct" of its operations. The Animal Legal Defense Fund, the ACLU of Idaho, and the Center for Food Safety, among others, challenged the law in federal court.

In a straightforward application of First Amendment doctrine, the federal court in Idaho concluded that the misrepresentation provision criminalized protected speech. While lying can be criminal—as perjury is—the First Amendment protects lies that produce no "legally cognizable harm."[49] Idaho could not show that the misrepresentation described in the law would produce harm. Harm "caused by the publication of [a] true story is not the type of direct material harm" that can be forbidden.[50] The Idaho law "only targets speech concerning the 'conduct of an agricultural production facility's operations' while leaving unburdened other types of speech at those facilities."[51] The court found that the "underlying purpose is to silence animal activists," and for that reason the law also suppressed speech based on its content, which the First

Amendment does not allow unless the state's justification is "compelling."[52] The state argued that "the property and privacy interests of agricultural production facilities supersede all other interests." The court responded: "Given the public's interest in the safety of the food supply, worker safety, and the humane treatment of animals, it would contravene strong First Amendment values to say the State has a compelling interest in affording these heavily regulated facilities extra protection from public scrutiny."[53]

On appeal, the Ninth Circuit Court of Appeals in San Francisco partly reversed the lower court's decision. Press interests both won and lost. On the winning side, the court straight off recognized the importance of the case to the press even though the plaintiffs were not media organizations. "Investigative journalism has long been a fixture in the American press, particularly with regard to food safety," the court wrote, citing Upton Sinclair's 1906 novel *The Jungle*. The court said that the case "highlights the tension between journalists' claimed First Amendment right to engage in undercover investigations and the state's effort to protect privacy and property rights in the agricultural industry." And it added that it was "sensitive to journalists' constitutional right to investigate and publish exposés on the agricultural industry." But the court then added, as the Supreme Court has also said, that the right "to gather news . . . does not exempt journalists from laws of general applicability."[54]

The court next addressed the text of the Idaho law. It first held that the Idaho law violated the First Amendment by making it a crime to engage in "misrepresentation" to enter "an agricultural facility." Sometimes deception will be a legitimate investigative tool. On the debit side, however, the court wrote that the First Amendment does not protect misrepresentation when it is used to obtain the records of or employment with an agricultural facility. Last, the court struck down the statute's prohibition on making secret audio or video recordings of the "conduct of an agricultural production facility's operations." Idaho had argued that while the final video recording may itself be protected speech, the act of making it was not speech. "This argument," wrote the court, "is akin to saying that even though a book is protected by the First Amendment, the process of writing the book is not." The court refused "to disaggregate the creation of the video from the video or audio recoding itself."[55]

In Wyoming, advocacy groups would cross private land to reach public land in order to collect information about environmental and other harms, which they would then report to government regulators. To end that activity, the Wyoming legislature passed laws in 2016 making it a crime to trespass on private lands to collect information relating to land use and record where the information was gathered. This crime carried harsher penalties than did the law against simple trespass. The Natural Resources Defense Council and others challenged it. They argued that they needed to record the precise locations where information is gathered because regulators could not take corrective action unless they knew where to look. So they needed to cross private land to get to those locations. The Tenth Circuit Court of Appeals, based in Denver, said the Wyoming law violated the First Amendment's Speech Clause because it prohibited the advocacy groups from collecting information that would further public debate.

Two aspects of the Tenth Circuit's decision are especially relevant for the press. First, Wyoming argued that it was not limiting speech. It was only prohibiting trespass on private land, which is conduct, not speech. The court dismissed that argument. The law heightened the punishment for trespass when a person's reason to trespass was to gather information to include in speech. "The fact that one aspect of the challenged statutes concerns private property," the court wrote, "does not defeat the need for First Amendment scrutiny."[56] Second, the court ruled that the Speech Clause protected the *collection* of information as well as the speech that would later contain it. "Facts, after all, are the beginning point for much of the speech that is most essential to advance human knowledge and to conduct human affairs," the court wrote, quoting the Supreme Court.[57] Protection for the collection of information for the purpose of then including it in speech also describes newsgathering.

Despite the victory for press interests in the Tenth Circuit and the partial victory in the Ninth Circuit, these decisions are inconclusive. At the very least, they establish that even if the act of newsgathering has little or no First Amendment protection when it violates laws of general applicability, the First Amendment does prohibit the government from using the criminal law to single out newsgathering for heightened penalties. That conclusion, welcome as it is, turns on the precise wording of the challenged statutes. Guided by the courts' decisions, Idaho and Wyoming are free to try to rewrite their laws to avoid the constitutional infirmities the courts identified. Indeed, both courts recognized as much. How these or other courts will respond to more carefully drafted laws that aim to impede discovery of (possibly criminal) mistreatment of animals or environmental harm, or newsgathering more broadly, remains to be seen.

6

FOUR LEGISLATIVE CHANGES TO SAFEGUARD INVESTIGATIVE REPORTING

Much of this book relies on the First Amendment's Press Clause or judge-made (common) law as the source of rules to protect the work of the press. This chapter identifies four ways in which legislatures, especially Congress, can add to that protection. They are by spending public money for investigative reporting, adopting a national anti-SLAPP law, ensuring the opportunity for appellate review of adverse jury decisions, and strengthening freedom-of-information acts. SLAPP stands for "strategic lawsuits against public participation." An anti-SLAPP law enables courts quickly to resolve litigation against the press, saving time and money, and to order the loser to pay the press organization or journalist's legal fees and costs if the case is dismissed.

PUBLIC MONEY FOR JOURNALISM

Total ad revenue for newspapers (digital and print combined) fell to an estimated $18.3 billion in 2016, from an estimated $20.4 billion a year earlier and from $45.4 billion in 2007.

Circulation revenue increased only modestly, from $10.3 billion in 2007 to an estimated $10.9 billion in 2016.[1] Digital advertising revenue is steadily increasing but nowhere near enough to compensate for the decline in print advertising revenue. Between 2003 and 2014, digital advertising revenue increased from $1.2 billion to $3.5 billion. Print advertising revenue declined from $44.9 billion to $16.4 billion in the same period.[2]

Declining revenue has meant fewer jobs. The Brookings Institution reports that American newspapers employed 59,000 "journalists" in 1989. By 2012, that number had declined to 36,000.[3] The American Society of News Editors reports a decline in the number of "fulltime journalists" at daily newspapers from 53,600 in 2006 to 32,900 in 2015.[4] Pew reports 68,610 "newsroom employees" in 2006 and 41,400 in 2015.[5] The Bureau of Labor Statistics reports that newspaper employment in all positions dropped from 365,200 in February 2006 to 184,900 in February 2016.[6]

While the numbers vary depending on the source, definitions, and time period, downsizing and decreased revenue have been persistent, year after year. Further proof should not be needed to recognize that the old business structure for news organizations, one that contributed to the support of investigative reporting, is contracting. Nor can we predict now when or if new models will replace lost income and jobs. Even if we resist pessimism, optimism seems misplaced. The likelihood of a robust reversal anytime soon is low. And we can't wait. Faced with uncertainty, we need to find new ways for the press to pay for investigations in addition to its other work. What will these new ways be? The discussion is well underway. Much of it proposes new business models. But some of it, probably little more than a fringe at this point, envisions public funds. Yet public funds can distort objectivity without our knowing it. Even if it does not, it can appear that way. Defining the options for providing public support is easy. There are three. The government can take less money from for-profit press organizations by reducing their taxes. Individuals and foundations can finance the nonprofit press or particular investigations with grants and contributions. The government can give money directly to press organizations, journalists, and others. Any policy must protect the fact and appearance of independence. Most important, the government should have no discretion in directing how public funds are allocated or (the courts aside) identifying the tax law's beneficiaries, beyond the decision to allocate the money or to enact the tax changes in the first place. Safeguards to protect independence will be a special challenge if government gives money to the press, rather than taking less money from it.

A tax-relief strategy that frees up money for investigative reporting can take several forms. Most obvious is lower tax brackets for press organizations (which would require a definition of "press organization") or for the journalism of companies that also have other businesses (another definition). But that strategy cannot ensure that the money will go to investigations, which is my goal. It may end up in shareholder dividends or fashion and sports reporting. So another possibility is to allow the salaries and other costs associated with investigative reporting, or a percentage of them, to count as a credit on tax returns, with a cap on the amount. Press organizations will, of course, have to support any claim for this credit, but they must do so now when the same expenses are listed as business deductions. We would need a definition of investigative reporting, which the government, perhaps through the IRS, would administer. That in turn creates a risk of government interference or influence. On the other hand, the courts will be available to review IRS decisions that reject a claimed credit, as they now review other IRS decisions. Any tax-based plan needs a final adjudicator. It can't be the political branches of governments, and it can't be the taxpayer. So it must be the courts. This should not alarm us. The courts have long protected the press against liability claims that threaten its work. However, a tax solution has a more fundamental limitation. It will not help press organizations that are losing money or earning little. It will not help nonprofit media that pay no taxes. Letting press organizations keep more of their profits offers nothing if there are little or no profits to keep.

The second option for funding the press, which is available now, relies on private (including foundation) grants and contributions to press entities formed as nonprofit organizations. These organizations would engage in fundraising no different from what universities, museums, and other charities now do. A development staff would be needed. The Marshall Project and ProPublica are examples.[7] Earmarking will be a concern, but not if investigative work is all or nearly all the recipient does or if the grant is for an investigative category, for example, stories about the environment or education. Grants can also fund the work of book authors and independent journalists.

The prospect of changing the law to permit tax deductions for grants and contributions to *for-profit* press organizations (even nominally for-profit ones) is politically unlikely, at least in the immediate term.[8] Press organizations that are now for-profit could reform themselves as nonprofit entities. But editorial support for political candidates is forbidden to nonprofit organizations.[9] The law could be changed to allow nonprofit press organizations to endorse candidates,[10] but doing so would require a definition of "the press" and run the risk that courts will find the different treatment of other nonprofit organizations impermissible. The prohibition on political endorsements by nonprofit organizations could deter the legacy media from converting to nonprofit status. Furthermore, a nonprofit entity is not exempt from taxes for all income. Unrelated business income is taxable.[11]

The silver-bullet solution we want does not exist. Ideally, we want a way to provide funds for investigative reporting that (1) will not require congressional action, because what Congress (or a state legislature) appropriates in one year it can deny in the next; (2) will be efficient, which means the money will go where we want it to go; (3) will yield sufficient funds to help achieve our goal of sustainable and robust investigative reporting; and (4) will eliminate the risk of governmental interference with the subjects chosen for investigation or the content of publications. Achieving three of these goals with a single solution is possible, but none promises to satisfy all four. The prospect of public money risks government interference, yet it is potentially the most substantial source. Of course, the options are not mutually exclusive, so we can and should consider them all. Here, I will argue for, as part of the mix, indirect government funding, supplemented by taxpayer contributions and foundation grants, to support investigative reporting. My proposal is modest. The funds would be available only to nonprofit entities and to journalists and authors, although the work it supports could then appear in for-profit publications.[12] An independent body, described below, not the government, would choose recipients.

The argument for government funding—for giving public money to investigative journalists, authors, and nonprofit organizations—is controversial, even for those eager to find new ways to support the press financially. Leonard Downie and Michael Schudson in their 2009 study "The Reconstruction of American Journalism," while recognizing the financial need, write that they "are not recommending a government bailout of newspapers, nor any of the various direct subsidies that governments give newspapers in many European countries."[13] The qualifier here is the word "direct." The closest the authors come is this recommendation:

> A national Fund for Local News should be created with money the Federal Communications Commission now collects from or could impose on telecom users, television and radio broadcast licensees, or Internet service providers and which would be administered in open competition through state Local News Fund Councils.[14]

In their book, Robert McChesney and John Nichols have many suggestions for how to fund journalism in general, not investigative reporting in particular. Among the suggestions are lower postage rates, more money for public service broadcasting, conversion of failing newspapers to nonprofit status, and their "centerpiece," a "Citizenship News Voucher" through which "every American adult gets a $200 voucher she can use to donate money to any nonprofit news medium of her choice."[15] Their "first and most fundamental purpose is to prevent any direct control by politicians over editorial content."[16] Again, the key word is "direct."

The strongest argument against government funding for investigative journalism in any form predicts that it will compromise independence or, at least, the perception of independence. It could do both, of course, but it need do neither.[17] We know how to prevent or severely reduce the danger of improper influence. Today, Congress can and does provide that appointees to independent agencies can be fired only "for cause," such as neglect or malfeasance in office.[18] Federal agencies have inspectors general outside the chain of command, insulated against internal retaliation.[19] The solution is to create effective layers between the source of the money and the people who distribute it and to adopt structures that limit the ability of the former to interfere with the decisions of the latter.

True, Congress or a state legislature can always choose to cease authorizing funds. We might worry that the prospect of losing all or most government funding would influence the work of investigative reporters. But we should not reject what may make sense because it can be taken away. I also doubt the premise—that investigative reporters will compromise their work in order to keep the public money flowing.[20] Some strident predictions of lost independence are so unfocused and conjectural that it is hard to debate them. One opponent of using public money, criticizing the Downie and Schudson study, wrote:

> I've come to the view that the real protection of press freedom is in the idea of private property. Press freedom in Soviet Russia was lost precisely on this issue when, as American journalist John Reed told the story in his famous book, "Ten Days that Shook the World," a proposal was put on the table to restore the press freedom that had been suspended on the first day of the Bolshevik revolution. Lenin shouted it down with a diatribe about how that

would mean restoring to capitalists privately owned printing equipment, paper supplies and ink. [21]

What can one say in response? This is an argument based not
on facts but on a supervening ideology that defies discussion.
More measured skeptics do not explain why no barrier to
influence can work, although they seem to assume none can
if only because politicians can threaten to end subsidies.[22] That
threat, the argument runs, may not only influence recipients
and aspiring recipients but also whom the grantors choose to
fund, encouraging them to favor less controversial projects.
Those who make this argument cite the effort beginning in the
Nixon years to influence the Corporation for Public Broadcasting and the criticism of the National Endowment for
the Arts for making controversial grants,[23] even though both
have been in business for decades and, despite the occasional
skirmish, able to survive controversy. In any event, ways do
exist to face down defunding threats and to insulate the immediate grant makers—those who decide who gets support and
for what—from improper influence. Furthermore, the press is
quite able to discover and disclose those who might threaten
to reduce or eliminate funding because they are displeased
with the product.

Public, perhaps politically inspired, criticism of controversial arts grants should not lead us to anticipate the same
response when public money funds investigative reporting.
The display or production of provocative art can be used to
incite the public whether or not the art is publicly funded.
Telling a true story about corruption, threats to public health,
or abuse of power is not controversial, at least not in the same
way. The story may provoke controversy—which can be a
good thing—but if the story is written according to journalistic standards, it will be able to withstand criticism of its

very existence. David Schizer cites the "political firestorm [that] erupted in 1989 around NEA funding for the homo-erotic art of Robert Mapplethorpe, as well as for Andres Serrano's 'Piss Christ,' a photo of a small plastic crucifix sub-merged in the artist's urine."[24] But these events are too easy for politicians to disparage. Politicians can hardly criticize a story that reveals a defective consumer product that kills and maims or a story that reveals that a lobbyist paid for a government official's expensive vacation and that the official then sup-ported policies that favored the lobbyist's employer. The legiti-macy of funding will, over time, be further enhanced if the funded stories go on to win prizes and effect reforms that the public recognizes as valuable. In any event, to presume other-wise is to surrender confidence in the capacity of investigative reporting to matter in the long run.

Criticism of arts funding has hardly been a success story. Yet Seth Lipsky cites this criticism in arguing against Downie and Schudson's recommendation for funding local reporting through the FCC:

> I take no comfort from the analogy the authors of this report draw with government funding for the arts. In New York City, there came a time when the leaders the voters entrusted with their tax money concluded that what was being done with it in the arts was so abhorrent they tried to stop it. This happened in 1999, when Mayor Rudy Giuliani confronted the Brooklyn Museum over its dis-play of a depiction of the Madonna that had been splat-tered with elephant dung. A federal court wouldn't let the city stop funding the museum.[25]

It seems to me that Lipsky's claim self-destructs with his final line, even if we were to accept the likelihood of equivalent public or political outrage for a deeply reported investigative story. The museum exhibit prevailed over the outrage.[26] As often in American life, the judiciary will protect expression from political interference.

Let's say I am being overly optimistic. Let's say that some publicly funded investigative stories led to the sort of broad public hostility that transgressive art engenders. Imagine a story about global warming attacked by climate-change skeptics, who would do so anyway but can now add the fact of public funding to the charge. So what? The question is not will there be criticism but whether the prospect of criticism is a reason to be skeptical of, or even entirely to reject, a program of public funding. The possibility of criticism is baked into the job, whoever pays for it. We should expect public funding to survive, just as arts funding has survived, enabling the press to do more of what it exists to do—that is, give the public true information. That some will unfairly disparage the information and others will ignore it is unfortunate, but investigative reporting is not meant to be a popularity contest.

A proposal for government financial support for press investigations, including of government itself, raises several questions. First, why should the government do it? Can it defend the use of public money to produce a product that advertisers and readers may be unwilling (or less willing) to support as generously as they once did? Second, how can we trust a press investigation of government, or indeed of anyone, if it is government funded? The answer to the second question depends on measures that credibly insulate the press from the source of the money.

The justification for government funding rests on two propositions. First, press exposure of public and private conduct that is (or may be considered) wrong, hypocritical, abusive, harmful, or illegal (collectively, "wrongdoing") is necessary for democracy to work and is, therefore, a public good. The public should help pay for it. Financing should not depend entirely on uncertain subscription and advertising income or on foundation grants and contributions. As a public good, it should be broadly supported. John Coffee defines a public good this way:

> The key characteristic of a public good is the non-excludability of users who have not paid for it; people benefit whether or not they contribute to the costs of acquiring the good, in part because consumption of the good by one user does not diminish its availability to others. Public parks, public television, and the national defense establishment are all examples of public goods. Because people can "free ride" on others' payments, they have an incentive to underpay, even though they may consider these goods vitally important and would be willing to purchase them in the open market if they were unable to free ride. The net result is that public goods tend to be underprovided.[27]

Investigative reporting is a public good because its product—the story—is available to all, and use by one person does not diminish its availability (or value) to anyone else. All of journalism can be called a public good because truthful information about the world is good, but investigative reporting does more. It discloses public and private wrongdoing and can influence political choices. I use "political" in the broadest sense. Learning the disguised source of a political candidate's campaign contribution or that a company is selling genetically modified food mislabeled can influence voting or legislation and promote social policies that the public will deem worthy of support.

I not only distinguish between investigative reporting and all other reporting but also within the category of investigative reporting. Money is limited. Not all investigative projects will get government support. The harder it is to unearth facts, the more consequential the facts, the greater may be the value of the investigation. The major American cities with the dirtiest air should be relatively easy to identify. Identifying the people and policies causing it can be difficult to discover. Some investigations will prove more valuable than others because of their subject. Learning the truth about Abu Ghraib, Watergate, or Russian influence in the 2016 presidential election is more valuable to democracy than the disclosure that a local lawmaker took a bribe (limited value) or of a celebrity's love affair (no value). Some investigations may be largely or partly duplicative; others are unique. In deciding where the limited subsidies will go, someone will have to make choices based on these factors—value, difficulty, and novelty. They will also have to consider whether a particular project can attract support from a private foundation or a publishing house, newspaper, magazine, or other for-profit business.

The second proposition supporting government support of investigative journalism, beyond the fact that we should all contribute to a public good, is that the press needs the support to continue to do this work and, we might hope, more of it. Foundations and private donors will fund some investigative reporting. They are important volunteers, but they cannot be expected to provide an adequate and consistent level of funding. They will not compensate for the lost revenue of recent years. I suppose it could be argued that in fact they will, that anything worth supporting is supported one way or another despite the decline in press income and the shrinkage of their editorial staffs. Given the scale of the media's losses, that argument appears fanciful. But it is not necessary to debate this issue further; the reality and size of the need is not necessary to my claim. Even absent a present need, the first justification would stand on its own. The beneficiaries of this public good should contribute to its cost.

A partial analogy appears in much of what government now does. Building bridges, maintaining parks, providing public transportation, fixing roadbeds, funding libraries, and ensuring clean air and water are services government provides, some of which it could not be forced to provide. Governments routinely accept a legal obligation that they would not otherwise have to perform. Doing so may be politically necessary. Funding investigative journalism should also be politically necessary. However, unlike building bridges and maintaining parks, the duty to fund investigative journalism should be seen as embedded in, even if not mandated by, the structure of our Constitution. The press is an essential part of that structure—not all of what the press does, but certainly including investigations of illegal conduct and other abuses, or apparent abuses, of power by public and private persons. Adequate government funding for investigative reporting should be seen not as discretionary but as a government obligation. Funding this work should be no different from funding the judiciary, the Library of Congress, or the National Institutes of Health. It is an attribute of civil society—or our civil society, at any rate. The argument that funding for investigative journalism should be seen as a government responsibility must recognize that we lack a formal mechanism for ensuring that the government complies. No court will order it to do so, let alone determine the appropriate funding. That means that the obligation, unless contained in statute, is unenforceable, and possibly unenforceable even then. But not every political or even legal obligation will have a judicial remedy. If the responsibility is recognized, then as with funding for the arts and humanities, state and federal governments may be encouraged to fulfill it.

Am I creating something out of nothing? I expect that most legal scholars would say I am. A claim that the press is part of the structural Constitution is belied by the absence of any reference to it in the text creating the institutions of government—executive, legislature, and judiciary—and which together comprise the structure of government. The sole reference to the press, in the First Amendment, was added two years after the Constitution was adopted. That reference does not grant power or money. It protects the press against loss (abridgment) of freedom. While there may be overwhelming agreement that a free press is essential to our American democracy, nothing in the text of the Constitution says government must help support it. Government may have elected to assist the press in various ways—for example, with antitrust exemptions, postal subsidies, tax benefits, FOIA discounts, and press passes that allow access to locations closed to others—but doing so is discretionary.

This is a powerful rebuttal. If I had to rely on constitutional text or original intent, my claim would fail, although constitutional rights once dismissed as baseless have later been recognized, such as the right to use birth control, to have an abortion, and to marry a person of the same sex or a different race. I offer two arguments in reply. First, I am not making a traditional legal argument. The target audience is not the courts and need not include the courts at all. The judiciary is not the only institution able to implement constitutional values. My two audiences are lawmakers and the public. They should treat the obligation to fund investigative journalism as essential to the constitutional structure and our democracy.

Imagine a world where our knowledge of powerful public and private institutions and powerful individuals had to rely on what these institutions and individuals might choose to reveal or on the fortuity of leaks, which may at times, for strategic reasons, be inspired by the subjects themselves.

Second, to the criticism that I am creating something out of nothing, I reply that the Supreme Court did just that, beginning in 1964. As described in chapter 1, *New York Times v. Sullivan* and decisions in the ensuing decades broadened press and speech rights far beyond what original intent and the bare words "the freedom of speech, or of the press" could support. We crossed the "something out of nothing" bridge with those decisions, although it took 175 years to begin the journey. My argument for subsidies takes us further down the path that the *New York Times* line of cases cleared, a good deal further. These cases defined—invented, really—a new Press Clause. I am building on *New York Times*, as the Supreme Court did after 1964 to advance the nation's "profound national commitment to the principle that debate on public issues should be uninhibited, robust, and wide-open."[28] Of course, my argument is different in kind, not only in degree. I am advocating for government assistance to the press, not merely constitutional defenses against liability, as in the *New York Times* line of cases.

Ordering government to spend money to enhance a constitutionally recognized right may be unusual, but it is not novel. In 1963, *Gideon v. Wainwright* relied on the Sixth Amendment's constitutional right to counsel in criminal cases to require Florida to provide a free lawyer for an accused person who lacked money to hire one. Previously, the amendment was understood only to guarantee the right to have a lawyer, not to have one paid for by the state. No surprise—nothing in the amendment says the state must pay. Notwithstanding the absence of such language, the Court wrote that reason and reflection require us to recognize that in our adversary system of criminal justice, any person haled into court, who is too poor to hire a lawyer, cannot be assured a fair trial unless counsel is provided for him. This seems to us to be an obvious truth. Governments, both state and federal, quite properly spend vast sums of money to establish machinery to try defendants accused of crime. Lawyers to prosecute are everywhere deemed essential to protect the public's interest in an orderly society. Similarly, there are few defendants charged with crime, few indeed, who fail to hire the best lawyers they can get to prepare and present their defenses.[29]

Gideon was accused of a felony. Nine years later, the Court held that "no person may be imprisoned for any offense, whether classified as petty, misdemeanor, or felony, unless he was represented by counsel at his trial."[30] In 1985, the Court went even further, ruling that

when a defendant demonstrates to the trial judge that his sanity at the time of the offense is to be a significant factor at trial, the State must, at a minimum, assure the defendant access to a competent psychiatrist who will conduct an appropriate examination and assist in evaluation, preparation, and presentation of the defense.[31]

These cases require the state to fund legal and medical help so an indigent defendant can contest the state's proof. A lawyer and a psychiatrist paid by the state will be working against the state's goal of winning a conviction. The media, and especially investigative journalists, also monitor the exercise of state power (but not only state power).

How might public funding for investigative reporting via grants to nonprofit organizations and authors be structured to ensure independence? This is not the place to draft the details of a bill creating a "National Endowment for Investigative Journalism," as we might call it. But we can describe its main attributes. The structure of the National Foundation on the Arts and the Humanities, which includes separate national endowments for the humanities and the arts, offers guidance. The legislation creating the foundation says, as one of its justifications, that "Democracy demands wisdom and vision in its citizens,"[32] an observation that also justifies a national endowment for investigative reporting.

Consider the humanities endowment as the closer analogy. It is headed by a chairperson, appointed by the president with the advice and consent of the Senate. The chairperson has a four-year term and may be reappointed.[33] The National Council on the Humanities, consisting of twenty-six members, advises the chairperson, including on most grants. Council members serve six years and cannot be reappointed "during the two-year period following the expiration of [their] term." They are also appointed by the president with the advice and consent of the Senate. The council members must be private citizens with "established records of distinguished service and scholarship or creativity."[34] The president must "give due regard to equitable representation of women, minorities, and individuals with disabilities who are involved in the humanities."[35] Most important, the legislation also provides insulation from political interference. No federal agency or official may "exercise any direction, supervision, or control over the policy determination, personnel, or curriculum, or the administration or operation of any school or other non-Federal agency, institution, organization, or association."[36]

A national (or a state) endowment for investigative reporting would also operate through an intermediary body—let's call it a council—with a chairperson and the same caveat against interference. Here is one possible model.

Council members and the chairperson, all unpaid except for per diem expenses, will serve for six-year terms and be ineligible for reappointment. They will not be removable except for cause. Authority for funding decisions would rest with the chairperson and the council, which would have twelve members appointed by the president for staggered terms with the advice and consent of the Senate. Ethnic, political, gender, and experiential diversity should be required. Council members and the chairperson should be broadly recognized for distinction in the area of their work. Not more than half the council members may belong to the same political party. Eight members should have substantial journalism experience, but none should then be or recently have been employed by a news organization. None may then hold, or for the prior two years have held, a government position. The goal is to minimize the risk of conflict of interest. The endowment will have to adopt disclosure, confidentiality, and recusal rules. A professional staff with authority to make final funding decisions for limited grants within prescribed guidelines will further insulate recipients from the source of funds.

In some states, the governor or other appointing authority chooses judges from a list compiled by an advisory body. The same can be done here, further insulating the council and chairperson. An advisory body, which can consist of journalists, editors, academics, and others chosen by the president or governors, can nominate three persons for each vacancy.

Grant recipients must qualify as "the press," which means a promise to comply with ethical standards the council can develop. It will be the applicants' burden to satisfy the council that they will comply. Grants can be available to individuals, including book authors and documentary filmmakers. Nonprofit publications should be a rich source of applicants.[37] A collateral benefit of these grants—beyond the work they enable—is the opportunity they afford new generations of journalists to gain investigative experience.

With a structure like this, the claim that we lack the ability to insulate the endowment and its grantees from political influence is not credible. Politicians or others may seek improperly to influence grants (pro or con), but the kind of people I envision for membership on the council and as chairperson will not tolerate the effort. Importuning will not cause them to compromise their professionalism and independence if we choose wisely. Or let me put this differently. Those adamantly opposed to government support will always be able to construct a story, however improbable, about how efforts to insulate the granting entity and recipients from the source of the funds can be perverted. I don't deny that perversion of the process is conceivable. But the fact that we can imagine it (as we also can for arts and humanities grants) says nothing about its plausibility. If, as I believe, the risk can be made highly remote, the benefits to democracy and journalism make the risk worth taking. We'll know soon enough whether the idea will work because we will judge it by what it enables.[38]

Whether to support particular work and in what amounts will depend on variables the council will have to identify. Where the recipient is a publication, the variables would include circulation, frequency of publication, and funds available from other sources—sponsors, donors, and subscribers. Other criteria will be the credentials of the applicants, whether an organization or individual. What is their publication history? References can be required. The council will need to weigh the value—the importance to governance and the public—of the investigation the applicant proposes and the sum required to fund it. Perhaps most important, the council will have to define "investigative journalism." The endowment will be required annually to report all grants and the works to which they have led. The government's contribution to the endowment should be comparable to the appropriation for the National Endowment for the Humanities. In fiscal year 2017, that sum was $149 million.[39] Once the endowment is running, another source of its income can be foundation grants and individual and corporate contributions, which will be tax deductible. Taxpayers can be offered the opportunity to designate a portion of pretax income for use by the endowment.

I don't pretend that it will be easy to get a national endowment for investigative journalism off the ground, let alone fund it properly. It will be hard. It will take time. Strategically, it may be best to encourage an endowment at a local level in the expectation that success will inspire others and eventually Congress. I do know this: Anything not tried because it would be impossible will never get done, and some things that are tried in the face of impossibility get done anyway.

TWO INNOVATIONS TO PROTECT THE PRESS WHEN SUED

Anti-SLAPP Legislation and Guaranteed Appellate Review

In 2005, the Las Vegas casino owner Sheldon Adelson sued a reporter for defamation, then dropped the case after the reporter declared bankruptcy.[40] In 2006, Donald Trump sued the author Timothy O'Brien and his publisher, Time Warner Book Group, for defamation because O'Brien, Trump alleged, significantly understated Trump's net worth in a book. The trial judge ordered O'Brien to identify his sources, but the appeals court reversed, citing the state shield law.[41] A different trial judge then dismissed the case after concluding that Trump could not prove actual malice as required by *New York Times v. Sullivan*. Trump appealed and lost.[42] The litigation took nearly six years.

Wealthy plaintiffs can use the courts to get revenge whether or not their lawsuits are likely to succeed. Their lawyers may tell them that they will lose. They may not care. Lawyers for press defendants and authors may assure them that a defamation, privacy invasion, or other claim based on publication or broadcast is weak and nearly certain to lose. That is some comfort. But for the press defendants, the price of eventual victory may run to hundreds of thousands of dollars. They must pay counsel fees and discovery costs. There may be fees for expert witnesses. The plaintiff will incur these costs, too, but may not object if the primary or only goal is to punish a less affluent defendant. For plaintiffs like Adelson or Trump, the cost of suing may be small relative to their wealth. And readiness to sue can have a further value. If news organizations and others know that a person is willing to use the courts to retaliate in this way, they may hesitate to write critically about him or her in order to avoid a lawsuit and attendant expense.

In addition to financial cost, litigation can be taxing in three other ways. First, there is the time required to work with lawyers in preparing a defense. That is time away from work. Second, the defendant may have to submit to extensive discovery, including days of depositions. More time, including for preparation. Third is the psychological toll of uncertainty. Despite assurances of eventual success, no lawyer will guarantee it. The defendants may have to live for years through trial and appellate court proceedings, always with the possibility, however slim, of a substantial money judgment and reputational harm.

In most cases in American courtrooms, each party pays its own lawyers. With a few exceptions, winners cannot later recoup legal fees and other expenses from losers unless the claim against them was entirely without merit—that is, frivolous. Rarely will that be so. A victorious defendant may be able to sue the plaintiff for malicious prosecution after the case is over. But that will require a separate litigation, more time, and more legal fees. And it will require proof that the plaintiff lacked probable cause to sue, meaning that he could not reasonably have expected to win. Good-faith reliance on the advice of counsel can establish probable cause.[43]

The acronym SLAPP stands for "strategic lawsuits against public participation," which ordinarily means a lawsuit filed because of something the defendant said or wrote. Anti-SLAPP legislation enables the defendant to request a quick judicial dismissal of the case and reimbursement of its legal costs. Anti-SLAPP laws are available regardless of the plaintiff's motive, and they protect everyone, but the press is a principal beneficiary.

Thirty-one states, Washington, DC, and Guam have anti-SLAPP laws.[44] California is the anti-SLAPP leader. Its statute, first adopted in 1992 and amended since, applies when a person is sued because of certain acts "in furtherance of a person's right of petition or free speech . . . in connection with a public issue." Those acts include

(1) any written or oral statement or writing made before a legislative, executive, or judicial proceeding, or any other official proceeding authorized by law, (2) any written or oral statement or writing made in connection with an issue under consideration or review by a legislative, executive, or judicial body, or any other official proceeding authorized by law, (3) any written or oral statement or writing made in a place open to the public or a public forum in connection with an issue of public interest, or (4) any other conduct in furtherance of the exercise of the constitutional right of petition or the constitutional right of free speech in connection with a public issue or an issue of public interest.[45]

Although the language of anti-SLAPP statutes varies, one essential feature is a provision that allows the defendant to ask the court to take a quick look at the plaintiff's complaint and evaluate the likelihood that he will lose. The California law authorizes a judge to dismiss a complaint if she finds that there is no "probability that the plaintiff will prevail on the claim."[46] The court can reach that conclusion within months after the lawsuit is filed. Without this fast-track feature, the case could last years, with procedural delays, depositions, motions, hearings, and trial, all of which increase expenses and demand time. If the judge does dismiss the complaint, she must award the defendant its attorney's fees and costs.[47]

If every state had an anti-SLAPP statute as protective of First Amendment values as the one in California, we would be able to end this discussion now. But nineteen states have no anti-SLAPP statute. A plaintiff who wants to run up costs for a defendant and who has a choice can sue in one of those states. New Jersey had no anti-SLAPP statute when Donald Trump brought his lawsuit against Timothy O'Brien and Time Warner Book Group. Furthermore, courts in states that do have an anti-SLAPP law vary in their sensitivity to the free-press values the law is meant to protect.

The solution is a national law that will enable federal courts to apply anti-SLAPP features to claims filed in federal *or* state courts. Five members of Congress (two Democrats and three Republicans) introduced a federal anti-SLAPP law in the House of Representatives in 2015.[48] Hearings were held, but the bill never reached the House floor for a vote. The proposal defines a SLAPP suit as a "claim that arises from an oral or written statement or other expression . . . that was made in connection with . . . a matter of public concern." A matter is one of public concern if it relates to "health or safety; environmental, economic, or community well-being; the government; a public official or public figure; or a good, product, or service in the marketplace." This list encompasses pretty much anything an investigative journalist might choose to write or speak about.

Under the bill, if a news organization or journalist is sued because of a report on a matter of public concern, the judge must dismiss the suit unless the plaintiff can show that the claim "is likely to succeed." After dismissal, the judge must order the plaintiff to pay the defendant's "litigation costs, expert witness fees, and reasonable attorney's fees." As with the California law, the proposal contemplates a quick decision on whether the plaintiff will succeed.

The most significant part of the proposal is not, however, the introduction of anti-SLAPP benefits when cases are filed in federal court, important as that is. The most significant part of the law is that a defendant sued in a *state* court can "remove" the case to the local federal court and seek dismissal there, using the federal law's anti-SLAPP provisions. And this is so whether or not the state in which the lawsuit was filed has its own anti-SLAPP law. Removing the case means what it sounds like. The defendant can take the case out of a state court and transfer it to the local federal court for an anti-SLAPP ruling. If the federal judge dismisses the case, it's over, except for a possible appeal. The judge will order the losing plaintiff to pay the defendant's litigation costs. The effect of the proposed law is instantly to create strong anti-SLAPP legislation for the entire nation and to make it harder for an unhappy but affluent subject of a publication to employ judicial process as a weapon against writers and media organizations by suing in states with no or weak anti-SLAPP laws.

It can be a challenge to figure out why anti-SLAPP laws, though common, are not ubiquitous and why the federal anti-SLAPP bill has not passed the Congress. Resistance in Congress may reflect federalism concerns that oppose federal interference with state court jurisdiction. The failure of many states to adopt an anti-SLAPP law, or a strong one, is harder to understand. There does not appear to be a "no anti-SLAPP" constituency. Meanwhile, there is a constituency that supports the laws—media organizations—because they can predict being sued for what they write or say. Nonmedia defendants can also take advantage of anti-SLAPP laws, and they have, but those defendants, unlike the media, will not anticipate a need to do so routinely because of the nature of their occupations or businesses. Perhaps the lack of strong nationwide anti-SLAPP laws reflects nothing other than legislative antipathy to, or apathy about, the press in the holdout jurisdictions and those with weak laws.

*　　*　　*

In 2016, Peter Thiel, a Silicon Valley billionaire, funded Terry Gene Bollea's lawsuit against Gawker Media in a Florida state court. Bollea, better known as Hulk Hogan, claimed that *Gawker* invaded his privacy when it posted a sex tape on its website featuring Bollea and the wife of one of his friends. Bollea won a jury verdict of $140 million, which forced Gawker Media into bankruptcy and to close after publishing *Gawker* online for thirteen years. Thiel, whom *Gawker* had earlier revealed as gay, funded the suit even though *Gawker's* actions did not concern or harm him. He explained his motives to the *New York Times*. "It's less about revenge and more about specific deterrence. I saw *Gawker* pioneer a unique and incredibly damaging way of getting attention by bullying people even when there was no connection with the public interest."[49] Paying for someone else to go to court is perfectly legal, and the choice to do so can be beneficial because it enables people without resources to protect their rights. However, Thiel's motive was not only to benefit Bollea but also to hurt *Gawker*, even to put it out of business. Other rich funders may be motivated by animosity only. There is no rule against funding a lawsuit to get revenge so long as the funder reasonably believes that the lawsuit has merit, in which case it is not a malicious prosecution. But the absence of malice will not prevent application of an anti-SLAPP law.

Florida has an anti-SLAPP law, but it did not help *Gawker*. Bollea's lawsuit reveals a different gap in the protection for media defendants sued for something they publish or broadcast. In order to prevent enforcement of the judgments, Gawker Media had to post a bond of $50 million and could not.[50] That meant that the trial judge and jury had the final say on the question of liability and on the size of the damage award. Gawker Media's only realistic option was bankruptcy.

Yet the finding of liability and (especially) the size of the damage award may have been vulnerable on appeal. We will never know. The appeals court might have overturned the verdict or reduced the damages to an amount Gawker Media could pay and, in either event, allow it to avoid bankruptcy. Protecting the right to appeal by posting a bond is a common feature of American law and makes sense. In exchange for the right to appeal, the defendant's bond guarantees that money sufficient to pay the plaintiff's judgment will be available if the appeal fails. If there is no bond and the plaintiff is not allowed to enforce the judgment in the interim, the defendant might dissipate his assets. When the judgment is against a press organization or journalist, however, the Press Clause should be read to require different rules in order to ensure an opportunity for appellate review and to avoid cessation of publication and bankruptcy. Legislation can do the same. The trial court, subject to appellate review, should be required to weigh several factors in deciding the amount of the appeal bond, if any. These include the threat to First Amendment interests if the defendant cannot appeal; the strength of the appellate arguments and the likelihood of reversal either of the finding of liability or the damages awarded; the ability of the defendant to post a bond in an amount that will not force it to close or go into bankruptcy; what that amount is; the risk to the plaintiff, if the judgment is affirmed, that the defendant will then be in an appreciably worse financial position; and whether limitation on expenditures pending appeal, perhaps with a court monitor, can minimize the risk of dissipation of assets.

Here's an analogy. When a person, free on bail, is convicted of a crime, she may ask the court to continue bail during her appeal rather than remand her to prison immediately.

In ruling, the court will consider the strength of the defendant's legal arguments to reverse the conviction and the likelihood that she will flee in the interim. If the legal arguments are strong and the risk of flight negligible, the court may be disposed to grant affordable bail pending appeal and thereby avoid months of incarceration of a defendant who may eventually be exonerated. The defendant can ask a higher court to review a trial judge's refusal of bail on appeal.

The *Gawker* episode is comparable. If a media company has legal arguments to reverse a finding of liability for what it published or to reduce the amount of damages, the courts should adjust the size of any required bond to ensure the opportunity for appellate review.

Improving the Freedom of Information Act

The federal, state, and local governments hold large quantities of information that can be divided into four unequal groups. One group contains information that should not be public. Secrecy is justified, for example, for personnel records, tax returns, and matters of national security. While there is consensus that this group is appropriate, there will be disagreement on its breadth. A second group consists of information that the government has made public, without request or in response to an inquiry, possibly through the federal or a state freedom-of-information act. A third group contains information that the government has not disclosed but would if asked. In a final group, the most important for my purposes, is information that the government has refused (or would refuse) to release in response to a FOIA request. Nine categories of information are excluded from the federal

FOIA's reach. The government may claim that the requested information is within one of the exceptions. If challenged, a court will be asked to rule. The government may also simply ignore a request. A court may then be asked to address the government's failure to respond. If the government loses in court, it can be ordered to pay the requester's attorney's fees.

The federal FOIA favors the "news media," a term it defines. The news media is relieved of charges for searching for requested documents and must pay only duplication costs (which won't exist if the transmittal is electronic). Even those costs may be reduced or eliminated "if disclosure of the information is in the public interest because it is likely to contribute significantly to public understanding of the operations or activities of the government and is not primarily in the commercial interest of the requester."[51] This is a burden the news media will often satisfy.

The federal act also requires government agencies to adopt rules for expedited responses when the person making the request has a "compelling need," which means "with respect to a request made by a person primarily engaged in disseminating information, *urgency* to inform the public concerning actual or alleged Federal Government activity."[52] Federal agencies may entertain additional, narrow reasons for expedition.[53]

The word "urgency" and the way it has been construed are unacceptable impediments when the requester is a journalist or news organization. The Justice Department's regulations interpret the word to set too high a bar.[54] The department quotes case authority saying that in order "to determine if 'urgency to inform' exists, a court must consider whether [the] request concerns 'matter of current exigency to the American public,' whether consequences of delaying response would 'compromise a significant recognized interest,' whether [the] request concerns 'federal government activity,' and 'credibility of [the] requester.'"[55] It further cites authority requiring that the request be "the subject of [a] breaking news story."[56] And it relies on a narrow interpretation of the statutory phrase "compelling need."[57] The Defense Department says "urgently needed means that the information has a particular value that will be lost if not disseminated quickly. Ordinarily this means a breaking news story of general public interest."[58]

These tests substitute the judgment of government officials for the judgment of editors. They allow agencies to reject expedited disclosure because the request is not about a subject in the headlines. Yet press requests may not simply react to breaking stories but instead seek information for a story then in preparation, possibly long in preparation, and which may create headlines when published, possibly imminently. Even if publication is not imminent, a request may be urgent for other reasons. An investigation may be at a critical stage, and the requested documents may determine how, even whether, it proceeds.

Editorial judgment should presumptively establish the urgency of a request without agency second-guessing. Indeed, we would do well to eliminate the word "urgency" from the statute to make it clear that agencies may not assess the news value of the requested information, something agencies often cannot know when they are not aware of the story of which the information may become a part or which it will help shape. And the news organization should not have to explain. We should assume that editorial claims of a present need for the information are true. Editors, of course, should make these claims sparingly. There is also no reason why the timing cannot be the product of negotiation. The issue here is timing, not whether the requested information is exempt from disclosure.

While the federal and state FOI acts often work well, two additional problems make their use by news media less valuable than they could and should be. First, lack of a timely response to a request, or an indefensible denial, can result in not getting information or getting it after the need has passed. The remedy of going to court will have little or no value if victory will come too late for the disclosure to be useful or as useful. Second, the provision allowing courts to order the government to pay the successful plaintiff's legal costs has loopholes that should be closed. Solving the second problem will ameliorate the first one by making improper denial or delay costly to the agency.

The federal FOIA does recognize the need for timeliness. When an agency receives a request for expedited review, it must inform "the person making the request within 10 days after date of the request" whether it is granted.[59] If the agency denies the request or fails to address it "in a timely manner," the requester can seek court review.[60] However, nothing in the act requires the court to treat the case expeditiously.[61] That should be changed.

It is the prospect of substantial legal costs that presents the greatest need for reform. Today, the press may win in court yet have to pay all or some of the costs of victory, including its lawyers' fees, which can be substantial and discourage court action. A government agency that realizes that uncertain legal costs may discourage a requester to go to court can choose to be unaccommodating and avoid disclosures that reflect badly on the agency, maybe on the very officials participating in the decision or their colleagues or superiors. The requester may not have the funds to pay a lawyer, and lawyers may be unwilling to take the risk that, even if successful, the court will award no fee or an inadequate fee. All FOIA requesters have an interest in timeliness and in reimbursement of legal costs, of course, although those with a commercial interest in information may care less about legal costs. The press, however, is seeking information for public dissemination, not commercial use or curiosity, which sets it apart. While the press, scholars, and book authors will fare better in court than others,[62] recoupment of legal fees is not guaranteed even if they prevail. Even affluent news organizations may be disinclined to seek court assistance if they must pay their own legal costs. Small-circulation newspapers, book authors, freelance reporters, and scholars will be especially discouraged. Unfortunately, judicial fee-shifting authority in the federal and some state acts is beset with qualifications that make the promise of legal fees unpredictable, which in turn discourages going to court.

Some state acts, including those in California, Florida, Illinois, and Texas, mandate payment of the successful plaintiff's legal fees with no or little discretion whether to award fees but with discretion as to amount. These states use the word "shall" in describing the duty of the court. For example, Florida law provides:

> If a civil action is filed against an agency to enforce the provisions of this chapter, the court *shall* assess and award the reasonable costs of enforcement, including reasonable attorney fees, against the responsible agency if the court determines that . . . the agency unlawfully refused to permit a public record to be inspected or copied.[63]

But the federal FOIA uses the word "may," not "shall." "The court *may* assess against the United States reasonable attorney fees and other litigation costs reasonably incurred in any case under this section in which the complainant has substantially prevailed."[64]

New York's act says a court "may" award attorney fees and other costs but only when "the agency had no reasonable basis for denying access."[65] The New York condition undermines the goal of fee shifting. The successful plaintiff must anticipate the possibility of having to pay its legal costs unless the state's refusal was legally unreasonable. The state's lawyer need only think of a plausible reason for rejecting an FOIA request, not a winning one, and lawyers are nothing if not imaginative. The federal act does not have this condition (or any other specific factor) in its text, but a 1973 Senate report does contain four criteria for deciding whether to award a fee. The courts have adopted these criteria as a guide. In an influential opinion, the federal appeals court in New Orleans wrote:

> The original senate bill had listed four criteria for the award of attorneys' fees to plaintiffs who substantially prevailed: [1] the benefit to the public deriving from the case, [2] the commercial benefit to the complainant and [3] the nature of his interest in the federal records sought, and [4] whether the government's withholding of the record sought had a reasonable basis in law.[66]

Nor are these criteria exclusive. The same court said "the district court is of course free to take into account equitable factors in addition to the four criteria discussed above."[67]

The Senate report recognized that the prospect of legal costs could deter all but the most affluent news organizations from challenging a government agency's refusal to provide information or a failure to respond in a timely manner. It quoted the National Newspaper Association:

> An overriding factor in the failure of our segment of the Press to use the existing Act is the expense connected with litigating FOIA matters in the courts once an agency has decided against making information available. This is probably the most undermining aspect of existing law and severely limits the use of the FOI Act by all media, but especially smaller sized newspapers. The financial expense involved, coupled with the inherent delay in obtaining the information means that very few community newspapers are ever going to be able to make use of the Act unless changes are initiated by the Committee.[68]

The Senate report emphasized the preferred position of news organizations:

> A court would ordinarily award fees, for example, where a newsman was seeking information to be used in a publication or a public interest group was seeking information to further a project benefitting the general public, but it would not award fees if a business was using the FOIA to obtain data relating to a competitor or as a substitute for discovery in private litigation with the government.[69]

Echoing this language, courts have concurred in favoring awards when, as the federal appeals court in San Francisco has written, the plaintiff's "interest in the information sought was scholarly or journalistic or public-oriented."[70]

Conditioning legal costs on an assessment of "whether the government's withholding of the record sought had a reasonable basis in law," as the federal appeals court in New Orleans did and the 1973 Senate report proposed, can appear fair on first impression. If the agency has researched the question—or its lawyers have—and reasonably concluded that one of the nine exemptions from the reach of the FOIA applied, then it hasn't been obstructionist, nor (let us assume) has it withheld the information in order to avoid embarrassment or liability. It has done so to comply with the FOIA, namely, the provision that certain categories of information are exempt for reasons of public policy. Why should the agency be penalized—by requiring it to pay legal costs that may come out of its budget—when it has made a good-faith if mistaken effort to research, interpret, and uphold the law?

That question seems to explain why the Department of Justice guidelines have quite an expansive view of what can count as a "reasonable basis" to reject an FOIA request. As the Justice Department sees it, a decision to withhold may be reasonable even with no supporting authority so long as there is no contrary authority that "directly" contradicts it. In a lengthy guide to the federal act for use by all federal agencies, the department wrote: "In general, an agency's legal basis for withholding has been found 'reasonable' if pertinent authority exists to support the claimed exemption. *Even in the absence of supporting authority*, withholding has been found to be 'reasonable' where no precedent directly contradicted the agency's position."[71]

The error in this argument is in thinking of FOIA fee shifting as a penalty for obstructionist conduct, just as courts may impose attorney fees for violations of a procedural rule or for frivolous claims. Consequently, if a denial is reasonable, there should be no fee. Whatever the merits of that thinking when the requester is not a news organization, it has none when a news organization is making the request. Then we should view fee shifting as merely an allocation of costs between two parties, neither of whom may be at fault and both of whom may be acting in good faith. A court will have decided that the news organization (or author, scholar, or journalist) is entitled to the withheld information. The requester should not have to pay a lawyer to get what a court concludes it was legally entitled to receive. This is not about blame. It is about making vindication of the right to information under the statute as cost-free as possible when the requester is the press.

For at least four reasons, news organizations (including authors and scholars) should be entitled to legal fees as a matter of right and regardless of the government's good faith in having denied the request. First, news organizations can be expected often to invoke an FOI act. They are in the business of gathering information. Most FOIA requesters are not. Commercial enterprises may be repeat players, too, but unlike news organizations, they are looking to exploit the information for profit and will not be deterred by having to pay a lawyer. Second, unlike commercial requesters, news organizations, authors, and scholars will use the information in a published story or study. They are acting for the public. Third, the information will be part of a story, study, or book that contains independent reporting or analysis. It will not simply be resold. Fourth, and perhaps most important, editors, reporters, authors, and scholars embody the Press Clause. Their work fulfills its promises and values.

Unlike the Supreme Court, which cited the difficulty in defining the press in declining to recognize a reporter's privilege to refuse to disclose the identity of a source, the drafters of the federal FOIA had no such trouble. As quoted in part in chapter 2, the FOIA easily defines "representative of the news media" in connection with entitlement to a reduced fee schedule:

> In this clause, the term "a representative of the news media" means any person or entity that gathers information of potential interest to a segment of the public, uses its editorial skills to turn the raw materials into a distinct work, and distributes that work to an audience. In this clause, the term "news" means information that is about current events or that would be of current interest to the public. . . . As methods of news delivery evolve (for example, the adoption of the electronic dissemination of newspapers through telecommunications services), such alternative media shall be considered to be news-media entities.[72]

The definition also includes freelance journalists, by contrast with those state shield laws that define a journalist as a full-time news media employee. "A freelance journalist," the act tells us, "shall be regarded as working for a news-media entity if the journalist can demonstrate a solid basis for expecting publication through that entity, whether or not the journalist is actually employed by the entity."[73]

It is not possible to know the extent to which the prospect of having to pay unreimbursed legal fees has caused news organizations, journalists, authors, and others whose requests are denied to refrain from going to court. Choosing not to go to court for this reason does not register on any data compilation. Even if a news organization or others can be confident of success in court, the federal act's fee-shifting provision also requires that the success be "substantial," a term that gives courts much leeway to deny or severely to reduce fees. Appellate courts say that whether to award legal fees and in what amount is within the discretion of trial judges, which means an appellate court will ordinarily defer to what the trial judge decided.

Civil rights cases provide an analogy. A plaintiff who proves that the government violated his constitutional rights will be entitled to have the government pay his legal costs even if the costs far exceed the plaintiff's recovery. This is because enforcing the promise of the various civil rights laws is seen to produce a nonmonetary benefit to society as a whole. By paying the plaintiff's legal costs, we encourage lawyers to bring these cases, while accepting the risk that a loss will produce no fee at all. The government cannot avoid paying the fee by claiming that its conduct had "a reasonable basis in law" and that it acted in good faith.[74] "When a plaintiff succeeds in remedying a civil rights violation," the Supreme Court wrote in 2011, "he serves as a 'private attorney general,' vindicating a policy that Congress considered of the highest priority."[75] Vindicating the promises of the Press Clause through FOIA litigation should be seen as having equivalent value. The legal cost of an erroneous, even if well-intentioned, denial of information should be borne by the government when the request comes from the press. Like civil rights lawyers, the press is protecting the public interest, not acting for its own narrow purposes.

IN CONCLUSION

Potter Stewart's Truth

O n November 2, 1974, nearly two and a half years
after *Branzburg v. Hayes* rejected a reporter's privilege to refuse to identify a confidential source, Justice Potter Stewart gave a speech at Yale Law School. It was
then published in the *Hastings Law Journal*.[1] Although Stewart had dissented in *Branzburg*, his speech did not attempt to
reargue the case. That would have been impolitic. But he did
try to stake out an independent life for the Press Clause, whose
future he may (correctly) have viewed as imperiled. After
reviewing several First Amendment decisions, Stewart said:

> It seems to me that the Court's approach to all these cases
> has uniformly reflected its understanding that the Free
> Press guarantee is, in essence, a structural provision of the
> Constitution. Most of the other provisions in the Bill of
> Rights protect specific liberties or specific rights of indi-
> viduals: freedom of speech, freedom of worship, the right to
> counsel, the privilege against compulsory self-incrimination,
> to name a few. In contrast, the Free Press Clause extends
> protection to an institution. The publishing business is, in

short, the only organized private business that is given explicit constitutional protection.[2]

"Structural provision" is another way of saying that the clause is built into (part of the structure of) our constitutional system of checks and balances, no different from the three branches of government. The ensuing years have not been kind to Stewart's hope of constitutional protection for the press as an "institution." We cannot know whether today, with the advent of a robust noninstitutional and differently institutional press, Stewart would extend protection of the Press Clause beyond the legacy press of his time. In 1974, it would not have occurred to Stewart (or nearly anyone) to anticipate that question. But the term he used—"publishing business"—comfortably allows for inclusion of new forms of communication. And Stewart's emphasis on the press's function, not its organization, is reason to believe that he would have interpreted the Press Clause to include the newcomers.

In his speech, Stewart also spoke of the rise of "so-called investigative reporting and an adversary press, that is, a press adversary to the Executive Branch of the Federal Government."[3] He cited the press's work in the prior two years and also in the prior decade, which he called "the Vietnam years." He was speaking just three months after reporting by the *Washington Post* and others had led to the resignation of a president. "Only in the [last] two short years," he said, "did we fully realize the enormous power that an investigative and adversary press can exert."[4] Of course, this "enormous power" is nothing more and nothing less than the publication of true information, which by itself achieves nothing unless and until others are moved to act. The press did not remove Richard Nixon from office. His imminent impeachment did.

Stewart identified a conundrum. The work of the press, even when it gives its audience true information about abuses of power, information essential to democracy, is often unappreciated, even scorned.

> The public opinion polls that I have seen indicate that some Americans firmly believe that the former Vice President [Spiro Agnew] and former President [Nixon] of the United States were hounded out of office by an arrogant and irresponsible press that had outrageously usurped dictatorial power. And it seems clear that many more Americans, while appreciating and even applauding the service performed by the press in exposing official wrongdoing at the highest levels of our national government, are nonetheless deeply disturbed by what they consider to be the illegitimate power of the organized press in the political structure of our society.[5]

Within the constraints of the rules of decorum then expected of (and observed by) Supreme Court justices when they spoke publicly, Stewart made it clear that criticism of the press for the reporting that led to Nixon's and Agnew's resignations was mistaken. "It is my thesis this morning that, on the contrary, the established American press in the past ten years, and particularly in the past two years, has performed precisely the function it was intended to perform by those who wrote the First Amendment of our Constitution."[6]

Assaults on the press have become more severe even though—or perhaps because—the need for Stewart's "adversary press" has grown as concentrations of wealth, coupled with court decisions equating money with speech, have led to the monetization of democracy. At the same time,

accusations of "fake news" by Donald Trump and others aim
to weaken the credibility of news stories that contradict their
facts and arguments. Yet despite the "fake news" claims, trust
in the press, never high, rose in 2017. Gallup reports that
27 percent of Americans in 2017 had "a great deal" or "quite a
lot" of confidence in newspapers and that 24 percent had the
same level of confidence in television news. These numbers
are up from 20 percent and 18 percent, respectively, since 2016
but lower than their historical highs of 39 percent for newspapers in 1990 and 48 percent for television in 1993.[7] Democrats and Republicans divide when asked if "national news
organizations" are "trustworthy." In 2017, 34 percent of Democrats said that national news organizations were trustworthy, up from 27 percent in 2016. Equivalent numbers for
Republicans move in the opposite direction—15 percent of
Republicans found national news organizations trustworthy
in 2016; 11 percent did so a year later.[8]

Can there be more dramatic proof of the wide chasm
between the work of investigative reporters, on one hand, and
the public's support for that work, on the other, than the jury's
1996 verdict in *Food Lion, Inc. v. Capital Cities/ABC, Inc.*,
discussed in chapter 5? ABC's

> broadcast included, for example, videotape that appeared
> to show Food Lion employees repackaging and redating
> fish that had passed the expiration date, grinding expired
> beef with fresh beef, and applying barbeque sauce to chicken
> past its expiration date in order to mask the smell and sell it
> as fresh in the gourmet food section. The program included
> statements by former Food Lion employees alleging even
> more serious mishandling of meat at Food Lion stores
> across several states.[9]

Food Lion made no claim that the broadcast was untrue. Members of the same community from which the jurors were drawn were Food Lion shoppers. We might therefore have expected the jury to be grateful for the information ABC broadcast.

It was not. After finding ABC and its reporters guilty of fraud, trespass, and disloyalty and awarding $1,402 in actual damages, the jury gave Food Lion an additional $5,545,750 in punitive damages (which the trial judge substantially reduced and the appellate court entirely eliminated). In other words, the jurors wanted to punish ABC—that's what punitive damages are meant to do—for telling Food Lion shoppers the truth about the adulterated food Food Lion was selling them. The punitive damage award was discretionary. Even if the jurors felt obligated, in light of the judge's instructions on the law, to award the modest actual damages they did, nothing required them to add punitive damages, let alone such a large sum.[10]

We might predict the opposite. Transparency in what the press does has never been greater. In several ways, the press invites or is subject to the public's evaluation of its performance. Most of these ways are new. Beyond letters to the editor, there are corrections pages, public editors or ombudspersons, comments posted on a news organization's website, and reporters who cover the media, their own publications included. Online news organizations compete with the legacy press to break stories. Critics are eager and able to grade media performance on the web and in print. This is all to the good. It has improved reporting. But it does not seem to have inspired broad confidence in the press. Blaming the press for the nation's problems is, unfortunately, a reality we must abide. And ignore. That will require legal protections and financial support for the press, which in turn depends on the aid of judges and lawmakers. But as I wrote in the introduction, we cannot rely on lawmakers and judges primarily. This book is meant to engage the public and especially reporters and editors in the governance questions it addresses. Although my focus has been on the meaning of the Press Clause, which is contained in the Constitution, a legal document, the answers to those questions are only incidentally legal. The meaning of the Press Clause must come from a broader consensus about the importance of journalism to democracy.

NOTES

INTRODUCTION

1. Burt Neuborne, *Madison's Music: On Reading the First Amendment* (New York: The New Press, 2015), 125.
2. *Janklow v. Newsweek, Inc.*, 788 F.2d 1300, 1306 (8th Cir. 1986).
3. Richard Tofel, "Non-Profit Journalism: Issues Around Impact," http://s3.amazonaws.com/propublica/assets/about/LFA_ProPublica-white-paper_2.1.pdf.
4. See http://www.pulitzer.org/prize-winners-by-category/206.

1. WHAT DOES THE PRESS CLAUSE MEAN?

1. Sonja West, "Awakening the Press Clause," *UCLA Law Review* 58 (2011): 1025, 1033. West cites Frederick Schauer, "Toward an Institutional First Amendment," *Minnesota Law Review* (2005): 1256, 1257: "something of importance is captured in the way existing First Amendment doctrine renders the Press Clause redundant and thus irrelevant, with the institutional press being treated simply as another speaker."
2. David Anderson, "The Origins of the Press Clause," *UCLA Law Review* 30 (1983): 455, 533.
3. Leonard Levy, *Legacy of Suppression: Freedom of Speech and Press in Early American History* (Cambridge, MA: Belknap, 1960).
4. Anderson, "The Origins of the Press Clause," 495: "Levy interprets the phrase 'freedom of the press' as a mere prohibition against restraints in advance of publication."

5. Leonard Levy, *Emergence of a Free Press* (Oxford: Oxford University Press, 1985).

6. David Anderson, review of Leonard Levy, *Emergence of a Free Press*, *Michigan Law Review* 84 (1986): 777, 783.

7. Leonard Levy, "On the Origins of the Free Press Clause," *UCLA Law Review* 32 (1984): 177, 180.

8. David Anderson, "Freedom of the Press," *Texas Law Review* 80 (2002): 429, 450–51.

9. Potter Stewart, "'Or of the Press,'" *Hastings Law Journal* 26 (1975): 631, 634.

10. Vincent Blasi, "The Checking Value in First Amendment Theory," *American Bar Foundation Research Journal* (1977): 521. In 2013, Pew Research Center reported that "about equal majorities of Republicans (69%), independents (69%) and Democrats (67%) view news organizations as a check on political leaders and there has been a significant rise in this view across nearly all demographic and political groups." "Amid Criticism, Support for Media's 'Watchdog' Role Stands Out," August 8, 2013, http://www.people-press.org/2013/08/08/amid-criticism-support -for-medias-watchdog-role-stands-out/. Those numbers changed four years later: "Today, in the early days of the Trump administration, roughly nine-in-ten Democrats (89%) say news media criticism keeps leaders in line (sometimes called the news media's 'watchdog role'), while only about four-in-ten Republicans (42%) say the same. That is a 47-percentage-point gap, according to a new online survey conducted March 13–27, 2017." Michael Barthel and Amy Mitchell, "Americans' Attitudes About the News Media Deeply Divided Along Partisan Lines," May 10, 2017, http://www.journalism.org/2017/05/10/americans -attitudes-about-the-news-media-deeply-divided-along-partisan -lines/.

11. Leonard Downie Jr. and Michael Schudson, "The Reconstruction of American Journalism," *Columbia Journalism Review* (November/ December 2009).

12. Not every story that is costly to report will be investigative. A story about life in New Orleans a decade after Hurricane Katrina may or may not be an example. Does it uncover official failures or misconduct? Or is it mostly descriptive? At the borders, people will disagree on whether a story is or is not a watchdog story. That doesn't matter for

my purposes. Policies that support investigative stories can also be available for other stories that some may put outside that category, as later discussed.

13. The Supreme Court had held that the amendment limits the power of the states as well as Congress by operation of the Due Process Clause of the Fourteenth Amendment. *Gitlow v. New York*, 268 U.S. 652 (1925); *Grosjean v. American Press Co.*, 297 U.S. 233 (1936): "The states are precluded from abridging the freedom of speech or of the press by force of the due process clause of the Fourteenth Amendment."

14. *Gustafson v. Alloyd Co., Inc.*, 513 U.S. 561, 574 (1995): "The Court will avoid a reading which renders some words altogether redundant"; *United States v. Menasche*, 348 U.S. 528, 538–539 (1955): "The cardinal principle of statutory construction is to save and not to destroy. It is our duty to give effect, if possible, to every clause and word of a statute"; (internal quotes and citation omitted).

15. *Williams v. Rhodes*, 393 U.S. 23, 30–32 (1968): "We have repeatedly held that freedom of association is protected by the First Amendment. And of course this freedom protected against federal encroachment by the First Amendment is entitled under the Fourteenth Amendment to the same protection from infringement by the States."

16. *NAACP v. Alabama*, 357 U.S. 449, 460–463 (1958).

17. *Borough of Duryea, Pennsylvania v. Guarnieri*, 564 U.S. 379, 388–389 (2011).

18. A debate among legal scholars is whether "the press" was only meant to describe a technology for communications—the printing press—and not the press as we know it today, not journalism, whether institutional or not. Eugene Volokh, "Freedom for the Press as an Industry, or for the Press as a Technology? From the Framing to Today," *University of Pennsylvania Law Review* 160 (2012): 459, 462–463 (contending that "the press" did not refer to an institutional press but rather to the printing press). Jack Balkin captures this duality in Jack Balkin, "Old-School/New-School Speech Regulation," *Harvard Law Review* 127 (2014): 2296, 2302: "The word 'press' has the dual signification of an institution for creating and distributing content and a technology for creating and distributing content. At the Founding it referred to the freedom to use the key mass communication technology of the day—the printing press. One may debate whether the contemporary meaning of

'press' should refer to technology or to the practice of journalism. But surely the two are deeply connected. Technologies enable certain practices of content production and certain organizational models, while practices of content production depend on the affordances of technologies and the support of institutions. Changes in what we now call 'journalism' have often been shaped by changes in technology and the economics of mass communication."

19. 558 U.S. 310 (2010).

20. *Id.* at 352 (emphasis added).

21. *Austin v. Michigan Chamber of Commerce*, 494 U.S. 652 (1990). *Citizens United* overruled *Austin*.

22. 435 U.S. 765, 782 (1978).

23. *Bellotti* then cites generic language from other cases for the uncontroversial proposition that the First Amendment protects all speech. "The press does not have a monopoly on its guarantees." *Id.* at 782.

24. 435 U.S. at 782.

25. 384 U.S. 214 (1966).

26. In addition to the Scalia dissent, citing *Bellotti*, the Kennedy opinion cited a dissent and a concurrence in *Dunn & Bradstreet, Inc. v. Greenmoss Builders, Inc.*, 472 U.S. 749 (1985). In these two opinions, a total of five justices expressed the view (though not as a holding of the Court) that the First Amendment protects nonmedia speakers as well as the press where an alleged libel is on a matter of public concern. These opinions do not support Kennedy's sweeping claim in *Citizens United* that the Court has "consistently rejected the proposition that the institutional press has *any* constitutional privilege beyond that of other speakers" (emphasis added). They addressed protections for nonmedia defendants in a particular circumstance, a category of libel cases, not *any* circumstance.

27. 384 U.S. at 215 (1966). One justice thought the Court lacked jurisdiction to hear the case.

28. *Id.* at 219.

29. 303 U.S. 444, 447 (1938).

30. *Id* at 447, 448.

31. *Id.* at 451. One justice did not participate.

32. *Id.* at 452. Kennedy cites *Lovell* in *Citizens United* for the proposition that the "liberty of the press is not confined to newspapers and

periodicals." 558 U.S. at 390 n.6. He ignores its endorsement of the importance of the press.

33. 384 U.S. at 218.

34. 420 U.S. 469 (1975).

35. *Id.* at 491.

36. *Id.* at 491–492.

37. 558 U.S. at 342.

38. 408 U.S. 665 (1972).

39. *Id.* at 681–682. Justice Powell, whose concurrence was required for the 5–4 *Branzburg* ruling, wrote that the "Court does not hold that newsmen, subpoenaed to testify before a grand jury, are without constitutional rights with respect to the gathering of news or in safeguarding their sources." 408 U.S. at 709. *Branzburg* is further discussed in chapter 4. There has been an ongoing effort ever since it was decided to treat Powell's concurrence, though necessary for the decision of the Court, as if it had been written in disappearing ink. It was not.

40. *Minneapolis Star & Tribune Co. v. Minnesota Commissioner of Revenue,* 460 U.S. 575, 583 n.6 (1983).

41. 408 U.S. at 703–704.

42. 376 U.S. 254 (1964).

43. For recognition that *New York Times* upended the common law and endorsement of the view that the meaning of the First Amendment's Speech and Press Clauses does change over time, we have Justice White's opinion for the Court in *Herbert v. Lando.* 441 U.S. 153, 159, 169 (1979). The question was whether a defamation plaintiff may in pretrial discovery ask about a publication's editorial process and its editors' states of mind in order to gather proof of actual malice. Although the Court held that the First Amendment did not bar the discovery, it reflected on the changes wrought by the *New York Times* line of cases:

> *New York Times* and *Butts* [discussed later in the text] effected major changes in the standards applicable to civil libel actions. Under these cases public officials and public figures who sue for defamation must prove knowing or reckless falsehood in order to establish liability. Later, [in *Gertz v. Robert Welch, Inc.*], the Court held that nonpublic figures must demonstrate some fault on the defendant's part and, at least where knowing or reckless untruth is

not shown, some proof of actual injury to the plaintiff before liability may be imposed and damages awarded.

These cases rested primarily on the conviction that the common law of libel gave insufficient protection to the First Amendment guarantees of freedom of speech and freedom of press and that to avoid self-censorship it was essential that liability for damages be conditioned on the specified showing of culpable conduct by those who publish damaging falsehood. . . .

It is not uncommon or improper, of course, to suggest the abandonment, modification, or refinement of existing constitutional interpretation, and notable developments in First Amendment jurisprudence have evolved from just such submissions.

44. 376 U.S. 254 (1964).
45. *Herbert*, 441 U.S. at 157.
46. *Curtis Publishing Co. v. Butts*, 388 U.S. 130 (1967) (plurality opinion).
47. *Philadelphia Newspapers, Inc. v. Hepps*, 475 U.S. 767 (1986) (also holding that a private person must prove falsity when the subject of the article was on a matter of public concern). In *Gertz v. Robert Welch, Inc.*, 418 U.S. 323 (1974), the Court went further. It ruled that a *private* person who claims he was libeled in a story on "a matter of public interest" must at least prove that the defendant was negligent. The Court then limited the damages that a private person could collect based on negligence to actual damages (lost profits, emotional pain). The common-law concept of presumptive damages in defamation cases—a concept that relieved the plaintiff from proving any harm at all because harm was simply presumed—was not constitutionally tolerable when a story was on a matter of public interest. To get more than actual damages, to get presumptive or punitive damages, the private plaintiff in a matter of public concern also had to prove actual malice. *Gertz* was a sharp break with traditional defamation doctrine, which had allowed private plaintiffs to win even if the defendant had taken great care to ensure that the defamatory statement was true.
48. *Florida Star v. B.J.F.*, 491 U.S. 524 (1989).
49. *Hustler Magazine v. Falwell*, 485 U.S. 46 (1988).
50. 532 U.S. 514 (2001).

51. In *New York Times Co. v. United States*, 403 U.S. 713 (1971), the Court refused to stop the *Times* from publishing the Pentagon Papers received from Daniel Ellsberg.

52. 475 U.S. at 477.

53. *Id.* at 779 n.4.

54. 497 U.S. 1, 20 (1990).

55. 558 U.S. at 352.

56. Even if the Court were to extend *Hepps* to require plaintiffs suing nonmedia defendants also to prove the falsity of a defamatory statement on a matter of public concern, thus eliminating the distinction between media and nonmedia defendants, it would do so on that issue only. It would not thereby have ruled that the Press Clause has nothing to offer the media.

57. 558 U.S. at 342.

58. Burt Neuborne, *Madison's Music: On Reading the First Amendment* (New York: The New Press, 2015), 6.

59. Thomas Emerson, *The System of Freedom of Expression* (New Haven, CT: Yale University Press, 1970), 6–9. Emerson's book is cited in many of the Supreme Court's leading First Amendment cases.

60. 435 U.S. 829, 838 (1978). Justice Stewart, concurring in the judgment, wrote that Virginia was seeking to "punish a newspaper." He cited the Press Clause. He would have upheld the conviction if the defendant were not the press. The majority relied on freedom of speech *and* of the press.

61. Opinions in two important cases underscore the risk, although neither resulted in press liability. They are *Bartnicki v. Vopper*, 532 U.S. 514 (2001); and *New York Times Co. v. United States*, 403 U.S. 713 (1971) (the Pentagon Papers case). *Bartnicki* is discussed further in chapter 5.

   The criminal law may be worded broadly enough to forbid the press from further dissemination of information learned from a government official or another source who has illegally disclosed the information to it. Although the *Times* was not prosecuted in the Pentagon Papers case, where the Supreme Court refused to enjoin publication, several justices warned that it could be. Harold Edgar and Benno Schmidt wrote in the *Columbia Law Review*:

Justice White was the principal author of the warnings. His opinion, joined by Justice Stewart, detailed a construction of [federal
criminal law] that would impose criminal liability on newspapers
for retaining defense secrets. He noted, moreover, that "the issue
of guilt or innocence would be determined by procedures and standards quite different from those that have purported to govern
these injunctive proceedings"—a clear reference to the traditional
wisdom viewing the first amendment as less of a restraint on send-
ing publishers to jail than it is a bar to the issuance of injunctive
relief against publications. Justice Stewart wrote for himself that
the criminal statutes "are of very colorable relevance to the apparent circumstances of these cases." Chief Justice Burger and Justice
Blackmun, in dissent, respectively registered "general agreement"
and "substantial accord" with Justice White's views, evidencing a
surprising willingness to speculate about matters extraneous to a
litigation which they complained had proceeded too hurriedly for
careful judgment on the relatively narrow questions briefed and
argued. Justice Marshall, while not approving the construction,
noted its "plausibility." With opinions reaching afar in such unusual
fashion, one may well ask "who won"?

Harold Edgar and Benno Schmidt, "The Espionage Statutes and
Publication of Defense Information," *Columbia Law Review* 73
(1973): 929, 935.

62. Kevin Q>ealy, "Election Facts to Keep Handy for Holiday Discus-
sions," *New York Times*, November 23, 2016.

63. Jose DelReal, "Voter Turnout in 2014 Was the Lowest Since WWII,"
Washington Post, November 10, 2014. For comparable percentages in
other years since 1960, see http://www.infoplease.com/ipa/A0781453
.html.

64. Pew Research Center, "Americans Spending More Time Following
the News," 2010, http://www.people-press.org/2010/09/12/americans
-spending-more-time-following-the-news/. These numbers may not
tell us much because poll respondents were apparently free to decide
what counts as news, a term that can include television listings, fashion, sports results, and traffic reports.

65. Amy Mitchell, Jeffrey Gottfried, Jocelyn Kiley, and Katarina Eva Matsa, "Political Polarization and Media Habits," October 21, 2014, http://www.journalism.org/2014/10/21/political-polarization-media -habits/.

66. Jeffrey Gottfried, Michael Barthel, and Amy Mitchell, "Trump, Clinton Voters Divided in Their Main Source for Election News," January 18, 2017, http://www.journalism.org/2017/01/18/trump-clinton-voters -divided-in-their-main-source-for-election-news/.

67. Pew Research Center, Newspapers Fact Sheet, 2017, http://www .journalism.org/fact-sheet/newspapers/. These numbers are not adjusted for inflation.

68. Scott Gant, *We're All Journalists Now: The Transformation of the Press and Reshaping of the Law in the Internet Age* (New York: Free Press, 2007).

69. Sonja West, "Awakening the Press Clause," *UCLA Law Review* 58 (2011): 1025, 1030. West makes the further point that by defining the Press Clause to protect only something called "the press," we are not thereby depriving others of constitutional protection for communications. The Speech Clause protects all.

2. WHAT AND WHO IS "THE PRESS"?

1. 408 U.S. 665 (1972).

2. 406 U.S. 205 (1972).

3. *Id.* at 215–216 (1972). Seven justices participated in the case, and six joined in this opinion. Justice Douglas dissented in part. He faulted the Court's failure to weigh the interests of the Amish children.

4. *Id.* at 235.

5. 408 U.S. at 704–705.

6. 811 F.2d 136 (2d Cir. 1987).

7. *Id.* at 138.

8. *Id.* at 142.

9. *Id.*

10. *Id.* at 144–145. Both quotes in this excerpt appear in *Branzburg*. The first one is from *Lovell v. City of Griffin*, 303 U.S. 444 (1938), as quoted in *Branzburg*.

11. *Von Bulow*, 811 F.2d. at 146.

12. *Chevron Corp. v. Berlinger*, 629 F.3d 297, 300 (2d Cir. 2011). Two law-
    yers employed by Chevron also sought the outtakes to use to defend
    themselves against criminal charges in Ecuador. *Id.*

13. *Id.* at 305.

14. *Id.* at 309. The court offered this hypothetical to explain its holding:
    "This distinction is perhaps best understood through an illustrative
    example. Consider two persons, Smith and Jones, who separately
    undertake to investigate and write a book or article about a public fig-
    ure in national politics. Smith undertakes to discover whatever she
    can through her investigations and to write a book that reflects what-
    ever her investigations may show. Jones has been hired or commis-
    sioned by the public figure to write a book extolling his virtues and
    rebutting his critics. Smith unquestionably presents a stronger claim
    of entitlement to the press privilege (which is not to say the privilege
    might not be overcome, depending on the circumstances). Jones, who
    was commissioned to write a book promoting a particular point of view
    regardless of what her investigations may reveal, either possesses no
    privilege at all or, if she possesses the privilege, holds one that is weaker
    and more easily overcome." *Id.* at 308.

15. *Id.* at 308.

16. *Shoen v. Shoen*, 5 F.3d 1289, 1293 (9th Cir. 1993) (citing *von Bulow*).

17. *Cusumano v. Microsoft Corp.*, 162 F.3d 708, 714–715 (1st Cir. 1998) (cit-
    ing *von Bulow*).

18. 5 U.S.C.A. §552(a)(4).

19. *United States v. Sterling*, 724 F.3d 482, 531–532 (4th Cir. 2013) (Gregory,
    J., dissenting in part).

20. *Id.* at 532 (Gregory, J., dissenting in part).

21. N.Y. Civil Rights Law §79-h. Here are key definitions from the New
    York shield law:

    > (6) "Professional journalist" shall mean one who, for gain or liveli-
    > hood, is engaged in gathering, preparing, collecting, writing,
    > editing, filming, taping or photographing of news intended for a
    > newspaper, magazine, news agency, press association or wire ser-
    > vice or other professional medium or agency which has as one of its
    > regular functions the processing and researching of news intended

for dissemination to the public; such person shall be someone performing said function either as a regular employee or as one otherwise professionally affiliated for gain or livelihood with such medium of communication.

(7) "Newscaster" shall mean a person who, for gain or livelihood, is engaged in analyzing, commenting on or broadcasting, news by radio or television transmission.

(8) "News" shall mean written, oral, pictorial, photographic, or electronically recorded information or communication concerning local, national or worldwide events or other matters of public concern or public interest or affecting the public welfare.

A restrictive shield law is not the end of the story. New York courts (and courts in other states) are not limited by their shield laws in the protection they afford the press. They can also rely on a state or federal constitutional privilege, just as federal circuit courts have, to give reporters greater protection than state lawmakers have provided in shield-law legislation. New York courts have done just that, citing New York State's constitution, among other authorities. See, e.g., *O'Neill v. Oakgrove Const. Inc.*, 523 N.E.2d 277, 280 (N.Y. 1988), where the state's highest court wrote: "We have no difficulty in concluding that the guarantee of a free press in article I, § 8 of the New York Constitution independently mandates the protection afforded by the qualified privilege to prevent undue diversion of journalistic effort and disruption of press functions."

22. In cases in which the federal court is enforcing a state law, a state shield law will apply but not in cases where the law is federal, including all criminal prosecutions. *Giuffre v. Maxwell*, 221 F.Supp.3d 472 (S.D.N.Y. 2016).

23. All quotations come from the text of the bill. The Society of Professional Journalists reported: "Government officials have attempted to jail and even bankrupt journalists to force them to reveal their sources or information they have gathered. A study conducted by Brigham Young University law professor RonNell Andersen Jones, for example, found that in 2006 alone journalists were served with more than 7,200 subpoenas from state and local governments, and about 800

from the federal government. Some news organizations are served more than 25 times a year, and most newsroom leaders perceived a continual increase in government action to compel journalists to talk."

In 2017, a bipartisan group in the House of Representatives proposed a less protective shield law. H.R. 4382, called the "Free Flow of Information Act of 2017," would, for example, cover only "a person who regularly gathers, prepares, collects, photographs, records, writes, edits, reports, or publishes news or information that concerns local, national, or international events or other matters of public interest for dissemination to the public for a substantial portion of the person's livelihood or for substantial financial gain and includes a supervisor, employer, parent, subsidiary, or affiliate of such covered person."

24. The act does not require the presence of a traditional editor supervising a traditional reporter. Such a requirement would limit the protection of the act to the institutional media. The covered journalist can be his or her own editor by exercising the editorial judgment the act requires.

25. 436 U.S. 547 (1978).

26. 42 U.S.C.A. 2000aa.

27. 42 U.S.C.A. §2000aa-6.

28. 42 U.S.C.A. §2000aa.

3. WHAT DOES THE PRESS CLAUSE DEMAND OF THE PRESS?

1. I realize that courts are likely to expect more from the institutional press than from bloggers, freelancers, or academic researchers because more is feasible. But each must operate under an appropriate ethical regime. Academics, of course, are working within a discipline that is likely to have demanding standards for proof and integrity.

2. The Code of Ethics of the Society of Professional Journalists and the Statement of Principles of the American Society of News Editors are a page or two long, but SPJ also publishes position papers and case studies.

3. The most impressive is National Public Radio's Ethics Handbook. In addition to explaining requirements in detail, it gives examples, including instances in which NPR itself failed.

4. 532 U.S. 514, 539 (2001): "Nor should editors, who must make a publication decision quickly, have to determine present or continued danger before publishing this kind of threat."
5. *Haynes v. Alfred A. Knopf, Inc.*, 8 F.3d 1222, 1232 (7th Cir. 1993).
6. *Shulman v. Group W. Productions, Inc.*, 955 P.2d 469 (Cal. 1998).
7. 955 P.2d at 479 (internal quotes and citation omitted). The court cited "The Right of Privacy: Normative–Descriptive Confusion in the Defense of Newsworthiness," *University of Chicago Law Review* 30 (1963): 722, 725.
8. 955 P.2d at 485 (internal quotes and citations omitted).
9. *Id.* at 488. The court quoted *Ross v. Midwest Communications, Inc.*, 870 F.2d 271, 275 (5th Cir. 1989): "Exuberant judicial blue-penciling after-the-fact would blunt the quills of even the most honorable journalists." The ruling would likely have been different if the station had televised footage of the naked body of one of the passengers. The Restatement (Second) of Torts of the American Law Institute states in a comment to §652D: "The line is to be drawn when the publicity ceases to be the giving of information to which the public is entitled, and becomes a morbid and sensational prying into private lives for its own sake, with which a reasonable member of the public, with decent standards, would say that he had no concern."
10. *Gaeta v. N.Y. News*, 465 N.E.2d 802, 805 (1984).
11. *Gilbert v. Medical Economics Co.*, 665 F.2d 305, 309 (10th Cir. 1981).
12. 955 P.2d at 489 (citation omitted).
13. The word "essential" in the final sentence of the excerpt in the text can be misread to say that without disclosing Ruth's identity, the station would be entirely unable to report a coherent story. This is not what the court meant. The word should instead be understood to say that courts will not substitute their view for an editor's judgment of what facts are essential to tell an engaging story.
14. 8 F.3d 1222 (7th Cir. 1993).
15. *Id.* at 1224–1225. Quotations are from Lemann's book: "'Luther began to drink too much. When he drank he got mean, and he and Ruby would get into ferocious quarrels. He was still working, but he wasn't always bringing his paycheck home.' Ruby got work as a maid. They moved to a poorer part of the city. The relationship went downhill. 'It got to the point where [Luther] would go out on Friday evenings after

picking up his paycheck, and Ruby would hope he wouldn't come home, because she knew he would be drunk. On the Friday evenings when he did come home—over the years Ruby developed a devastating imitation of Luther, and could re-create the scene quite vividly—he would walk into the apartment, put on a record and turn up the volume, and saunter into their bedroom, a bottle in one hand and a cigarette in the other, in the mood for love. On one such night, Ruby's last child, Kevin, was conceived. Kevin always had something wrong with him—he was very moody, he was scrawny, and he had a severe speech impediment. Ruby was never able to find out exactly what the problem was, but she blamed it on Luther; all that alcohol must have gotten into his sperm, she said.'"

16. *Id.* at 1231, quoting Luther Haynes: "'I know I haven't been no angel, but since almost 30 years ago I have turned my life completely around. I stopped the drinking and all this bad habits and stuff like that, which I deny, some of [it] I didn't deny, because I have changed my life. It take me almost 30 years to change it and I am deeply in my church. I look good in the eyes of my church members and my community. Now, what is going to happen now when this public reads this garbage, which I didn't tell Mr. Lemann to write? Then all this is going to go down the drain. And I worked like a son of a gun to build myself up in a good reputation and he has torn it down.'"

17. *Id.* at 1233.

18. *Id.*

19. *Shulman*, 955 P.2d at 481.

20. Federal officials found no basis to prosecute Janklow.

21. *Janklow v. Newsweek, Inc.*, 759 F.2d 644 (8th Cir. 1985).

22. *Janklow v. Newsweek, Inc.*, 788 F.2d 1300, 1304 (8th Cir. 1986). Despite the court's attention to the importance of editorial judgment, its decision turned on its conclusion that the alleged libel was nonactionable opinion, not an assertion of fact. But in reaching *this* conclusion, the court again emphasized the place of editorial judgment. "While the whole of the *Newsweek* article could not be classified as opinion or criticism, national newsmagazines nevertheless are not the same as local daily newspapers. The magazines have a tradition of more colorful, even feisty language, than do dailies; they are also required to condense to a few paragraphs those issues to which local papers devote

days of coverage and thousands of inches of space. Here, the magazine's generally freer style of personal expression and the article's transparently pro-Banks posture would signal the reader to expect a fair amount of opinion." *Id.* at 1304. If Janklow had won, as a public official he would have been required to prove that *Newsweek* was guilty of actual malice.

23. Using the word "continuing" would also lengthen the story because it would then have had to include a description of the origin of the prosecution.

24. Sydney Ember, "*Gawker* and Hulk Hogan Reach $31 Million Settlement," *New York Times*, November 2, 2016; Peter Sterne, "Gawker Media Files for Bankruptcy," *Politico*, June 10, 2016.

25. *Gawker* had argued that its posting of a brief excerpt of the tape was protected by the Constitution and that Mr. Bollea had given up his right to privacy by talking often in public about his sex life. "He has chosen to seek the spotlight," a lawyer for Gawker Media, Michael Sullivan, said. "He has consistently chosen to put his private life out there." Nick Madigan and Ravi Somaiya, "Hulk Hogan Awarded $115 Million in Privacy Suit Against *Gawker*," *New York Times*, March 18, 2016.

26. *Pittsburgh Press Co. v. Pittsburgh Commission on Human Relations*, 413 U.S. 376, 391 (1973).

27. *Id.* at 382–383.

28. *Columbia Broadcasting System, Inc. v. Democratic National Committee*, 412 U.S. 94, 98 (1973). A separate question was whether CBS's policy violated the Federal Communications Act of 1934. The Court said it did not.

29. *Id.* at 120–121. This language appears in a part of the opinion joined by two other justices. In that part, the plurality concluded that the station's decision was not government action subject to the First Amendment.

30. *Id.* at 124–125 (emphasis added). The Court relied on this precedent twenty-five years later in *Arkansas Educational Television Commission v. Forbes.* 523 U.S. 666, 674 (1998). A public television station had excluded a presidential candidate who had little popular support from an on-air debate, and he challenged the exclusion as a violation of the First Amendment. The Court rejected the challenge. It wrote: "Much

like a university selecting a commencement speaker, a public institution selecting speakers for a lecture series, or a public school prescribing its curriculum, a broadcaster by its nature will facilitate the expression of some viewpoints instead of others. Were the judiciary to require, and so to define and approve, pre-established criteria for access, it would risk implicating the courts in judgments that should be left to the exercise of journalistic discretion."

31. *Miami Herald Publishing Co. v. Tornillo*, 418 U.S. 241, 244, 258 (1974).

32. *Id.* at 258 (emphasis added). Especially noteworthy, the Court quoted *Government and Mass Communications*, the 1947 treatise of the First Amendment scholar Zechariah Chafee: "Liberty of the press is in peril as soon as the government tries to compel what is to go into a newspaper. A journal does not merely print observed facts the way a cow is photographed through a plate-glass window. As soon as the facts are set in their context, you have interpretation and you have selection, and editorial selection opens the way to editorial suppression." *Id.* at 258 n.24.

33. I do not mean to limit my argument to publications with a division between editors and reporters. Indeed, as developed hereafter, I will argue that a person writing alone (including the so-called lonely blogger) can exercise editorial judgment. The Press Clause also serves to protect, for example, book authors (like Lemann), scholars, and documentary filmmakers.

34. The role editorial judgment plays or should play in First Amendment jurisprudence is sparsely addressed in legal scholarship. One example is Randall Bezanson, "The Developing Law of Editorial Judgment," *Nebraska Law Review* 78 (1999): 754.

35. *Branzburg v. Hayes*, 408 U.S. at 703–704 (1972). *Citizens United v. Federal Election Commission* summoned the image of the blogger (though not lonely) to justify its reasoning: "Rapid changes in technology—and the creative dynamic inherent in the concept of free expression—counsel against upholding a law that restricts political speech in certain media or by certain speakers. Today, 30-second television ads may be the most effective way to convey a political message. Soon, however, it may be that Internet sources, such as blogs and social networking Web sites, will provide citizens with significant information about political candidates and issues. Yet, [the statute] would seem to

ban a blog post expressly advocating the election or defeat of a candidate if that blog were created with corporate funds. The First Amendment does not permit Congress to make these categorical distinctions based on the corporate identity of the speaker and the content of the political speech." 558 U.S. 310, 364 (2010).

36. The act "grandparents" freelancers with a defined record of working for the institutional press.

37. In this way, they are like prosecutors, who must decide which crimes deserve the attention of their limited resources. The client is the state, but the prosecutor decides what is in the state's interest.

38. Some ethics codes for journalists do speak of the need to be and appear to be impartial. Examples given are of conduct, like accepting gifts, that creates a conflict of interest. I subsume conflicts, real or apparent, under independence.

39. On the courts' insistence on independence where a documentary filmmaker unsuccessfully resisted a subpoena because he was not independent of his subject, see *Chevron Corp. v. Berlinger*, 629 F.3d 297 (2011), discussed in chapter 2.

40. *New York Times*, "Ethical Journalism: A Handbook of Values and Practices for the News and Editorial Departments," https://www.nytco.com/wp-content/uploads/NYT_Ethical_Journalism_0904-1.pdf, 8.

41. ProPublica Code of Ethics, https://www.propublica.org/code-of-ethics/.

4. PROTECTION OF CONFIDENTIAL INFORMATION

1. 408 U.S. 665 (1972).

2. Charlie Savage and Eileen Sullivan, "Leak Investigations Triple Under Trump, Sessions Says," *New York Times*, August 4, 2017.

3. *Branzburg*, 408 U.S. at 681. The full paragraph is: "We do not question the significance of free speech, press, or assembly to the country's welfare. Nor is it suggested that newsgathering does not qualify for First Amendment protection; without some protection for seeking out the news, freedom of the press could be eviscerated. But these cases involve no intrusions upon speech or assembly, no prior restraint or

208 ஐ 4. PROTECTION OF CONFIDENTIAL INFORMATION

restriction on what the press may publish, and no express or implied command that the press publish what it prefers to withhold. No exaction or tax for the privilege of publishing, and no penalty, civil or criminal, related to the content of published material is at issue here. The use of confidential sources by the press is not forbidden or restricted; reporters remain free to seek news from any source by means within the law. No attempt is made to require the press to publish its sources of information or indiscriminately to disclose them on request." *Id.* at 681–682.

4. *Id.* at 707. The full paragraph reads: "Finally, as we have earlier indicated, news gathering is not without its First Amendment protections, and grand jury investigations if instituted or conducted other than in good faith, would pose wholly different issues for resolution under the First Amendment. Official harassment of the press undertaken not for purposes of law enforcement but to disrupt a reporter's relationship with his news sources would have no justification. Grand juries are subject to judicial control and subpoenas to motions to quash. We do not expect courts will forget that grand juries must operate within the limits of the First Amendment as well as the Fifth." *Id.* at 707–708.

5. *Id.* at 682 (emphasis added).

6. *Id.* at 710.

7. *Id.*

8. *Id.* at 743.

9. *Id.* at 749–750.

10. *Id.* at 751. The lower court allowed for the possibility that Caldwell could be required to appear at the grand jury on "a clear showing of a compelling and overriding national interest that cannot be served by any alternative means." Stewart agreed but concluded that the government "has not met the burden that I think the appropriate newsman's privilege should require." *Id.* at 747. Stewart would have remanded the claims of the other two reporters for applications of the standards contained in his dissent.

11. *Id.* at 712.

12. 417 U.S. 843 (1974).

13. *Id.* at 844 & n.1. The policy provided: "Press representatives will not be permitted to interview individual inmates. This rule shall apply even where the inmate requests or seeks an interview. However,

conversation may be permitted with inmates whose identity is not to be made public, if it is limited to the discussion of institutional facilities, programs and activities."

14. *Id.* at 847.

15. *Id.* at 857 (emphasis added).

16. *Id.* at 863–864.

17. *Id.* at 859–860 (emphasis added).

18. 438 U.S. 1 (1978).

19. *Id.* at 10–11. The plurality wrote that *Branzburg*'s "observation, in dictum, that 'news gathering is not without its First Amendment protections,' in no sense implied a constitutional right of access to news sources. That observation must be read in context; it was in response to the contention that forcing a reporter to disclose to a grand jury information received in confidence would violate the First Amendment by deterring news sources from communicating information. There is an undoubted right to gather news 'from any source by means within the law,' but that affords no basis for the claim that the First Amendment compels others—private persons or governments—to supply information."

20. *Id.* at 32.

21. *Id.* at 17.

22. *University of Pennsylvania v. Equal Employment Opportunity Commission,* 493 U.S. 182, 201 (1990). The question before the Court was whether, in a case alleging discrimination in the denial of tenure, common law or the Constitution protected a university's peer review materials. A unanimous Court said they did not. Regarding *Branzburg,* it wrote: "In Branzburg, the Court rejected the notion that under the First Amendment a reporter could not be required to appear or to testify as to information obtained in confidence without a special showing that the reporter's testimony was necessary. Petitioners there, like petitioner here, claimed that requiring disclosure of information collected in confidence would inhibit the free flow of information in contravention of First Amendment principles. In the course of rejecting the First Amendment argument, this Court noted that 'the First Amendment does not invalidate every incidental burdening of the press that may result from the enforcement of civil or criminal statutes of general applicability.' We also indicated a reluctance to recognize a

constitutional privilege where it was 'unclear how often and to what extent informers are actually deterred from furnishing information when newsmen are forced to testify before a grand jury.'"

23. *McKevitt v. Pallasch*, 339 F.3d 530, 532–533 (7th Cir. 2003). *McKevitt* concerned nonconfidential sources.

24. Judge Posner wrote for the court: "It seems to us that rather than speaking of privilege, courts should simply make sure that a subpoena . . . directed to the media, like any other subpoena . . . is reasonable in the circumstances, which is the general criterion for judicial review of subpoenas. We do not see why there need to be special criteria merely because the possessor of the documents or other evidence sought is a journalist. The approach we are suggesting has support in Branzburg itself." *Id.* at 533.

25. *U.S. Dep't of Education v. National Collegiate Athletic Ass'n*, 481 F.3d 936, 938 (7th Cir. 2007).

26. Posner's opinion was explicitly rejected in *In re Special Proceedings*, 373 F.3d 37, 45 (1st Cir. 2004): "One distinguished judge has questioned whether *Branzburg* now offers protection much beyond what ordinary relevance and reasonableness requirements would demand, but our own cases are in principle somewhat more protective."

27. Neil Lewis, "In Closing Pleas, Clashing Views on Libby's Role," *New York Times*, February 21, 2007.

28. *In re Grand Jury Subpoena* (Judith Miller), 438 F.3d 1141 (D.C. Cir. 2006).

29. Compare Rule 3.8(e) of the American Bar Association's Model Rules of Professional Conduct, adopted by most state courts and federal trial courts and strictly limiting the ability of prosecutors to subpoena lawyers to provide nonprivileged information about current or former clients. Subpoenas are not permitted unless "the evidence sought is essential to the successful completion of an ongoing investigation or prosecution and there is no other feasible alternative to obtain the information."

30. 438 F.3d at 1162.

31. *Id.* at 1175.

32. *Id.*

33. Tatel wrote: "If litigants and investigators could easily discover journalists' sources, the press's truth-seeking function would be severely impaired. Reporters could reprint government statements, but not ferret out underlying disagreements among officials; they could cover public governmental actions, but would have great difficulty getting

potential whistleblowers to talk about government misdeeds; they could report arrest statistics, but not garner first-hand information about the criminal underworld. Such valuable endeavors would be all but impossible, for . . . sources who fear identification avoid revealing information that could get them in trouble." *Id.* at 1168.

34. *Id.* at 1176.

35. *United States v. Sterling,* 724 F.3d 482 (4th Cir. 2013).

36. *Id.* at 492. The court wrote: "There is no First Amendment testimonial privilege, absolute or qualified, that protects a reporter from being compelled to testify by the prosecution or the defense in criminal proceedings about criminal conduct that the reporter personally witnessed or participated in, absent a showing of bad faith, harassment, or other such non-legitimate motive, even though the reporter promised confidentiality to his source."

37. The court wrote: "Risen next argues that, even if Branzburg prohibits our recognition of a First Amendment privilege, we should recognize a qualified, federal common-law reporter's privilege protecting confidential sources. We decline to do so." *Id.* at 499.

38. *United States v. Sterling,* 732 F.3d 292 (4th Cir. 2013).

39. Matt Apuzzo, "CIA Officer Is Found Guilty in Leak Tied to Times Reporter," *New York Times,* January 26, 2015.

40. 724 F.3d at 528–529.

41. 28 C.F.R. §50.10.

42. "This policy is not intended to, and does not, create any right or benefit, substantive or procedural, enforceable at law or in equity by any party against the United States, its departments, agencies, or entities, its officers, employees, or agents, or any other person." 28 C.F.R. §50.10(j).

43. *In re Grand Jury Subpoena* (Judith Miller), 438 F.3d 1141, 1157–1158 (D.C. Cir. 2006). The judge identified state disparities:

> The state legislatures have dealt with this vexing question of entitlement to the privilege in a variety of ways. Some are quite restrictive. Alabama limits its protection to "person[s] engaged in, connected with, or employed on any newspaper, radio broadcasting station or television station, while engaged in a newsgathering capacity." Alaska's statutes protect only the "reporter," a category limited to "person[s] regularly engaged in the business of collecting or

writing news for publication or presentation to the public, through a news organization." The statutory privilege in Arizona protects "a person engaged in newspaper, radio, television or reportorial work, or connected with or employed by a newspaper or radio or television station. . . ." Arkansas's legislature has declared the privilege applicable to "any editor, reporter, or other writer for any newspaper, periodical, or radio station, or publisher of any newspaper or periodical, or manager or owner of any radio station."

Presumably, states such as these would provide the privilege only to the "established" press. Others are quite inclusive. The Nebraska legislature, for example, has declared:

> (1) That the policy of the State of Nebraska is to insure the free flow of news and other information to the public, and that those who gather, write, or edit information for the public or disseminate information to the public may perform these vital functions only in a free and unfettered atmosphere; (2) That such persons shall not be inhibited, directly or indirectly, by governmental restraint or sanction imposed by governmental process, but rather that they shall be encouraged to gather, write, edit, or disseminate news or other information vigorously so that the public may be fully informed.

> To that end, it protects any "medium of communication," which term "shall include, *but not be limited to*, any newspaper, magazine, other periodical, book, pamphlet, news service, wire service, news or feature syndicate, broadcast station or network, or cable television system."

Id. at § 20–145(2) (emphasis added; citations omitted).

44. *Jaffee v. Redmond*, 518 U.S. 1 (1996).
45. The act creates exceptions, for example, for information "reasonably necessary to stop, prevent, or mitigate a specific case of death, kidnapping, substantial body harm," or sexual abuse of a minor. Another

exception applies if the information "would materially assist the Federal Government in preventing or mitigating . . . an act of terrorism; or other acts that are reasonably likely to cause significant and articulable harm to national security."

5. PRESS CLAUSE PROTECTION FOR NEWSGATHERING

1. 408 U.S. 665, 681 (1972).
2. *Houchins v. KQED, Inc.*, 438 U.S. 1, 10–11 (1978).
3. *Richmond Newspapers, Inc. v. Virginia*, 448 U.S. 555 (1980) (finding a First Amendment right of the public, and the press as its representative, to attend a criminal trial); *Publicker Industries, Inc. v. Cohen*, 733 F.2d 1059 (3d Cir. 1984) (same for civil trials).
4. Restatement of Torts (Second) §158. Restatements of the law are developed under the authority of the American Law Institute, a prestigious body consisting of hundreds of lawyers and judges.
5. Restatement of Torts (Second) §652B.
6. Restatement of Torts (Second) §652D.
7. *Food Lion, Inc. v. Capital Cities/ABC, Inc.*, 194 F.3d 505 (4th Cir. 1999).
8. *Id.* at 510–511.
9. *Id.* at 511 (emphasis added).
10. *Id.* at 513.
11. *Id.* at 522.
12. 376 U.S. 254 (1964).
13. 194 F.3d at 522.
14. *Id.*
15. *Hustler Magazine v. Falwell*, 485 U.S. 46 (1988).
16. As the Supreme Court described it: "The inside front cover of the November 1983 issue of Hustler Magazine featured a 'parody' of an advertisement for Campari Liqueur that contained the name and picture of respondent and was entitled 'Jerry Falwell talks about his first time.' This parody was modeled after actual Campari ads that included interviews with various celebrities about their 'first times.' Although it was apparent by the end of each interview that this meant the first time they sampled Campari, the ads clearly played on the sexual double entendre of the general subject of 'first times.' Copying the form

and layout of these Campari ads, Hustler's editors chose respondent as the featured celebrity and drafted an alleged 'interview' with him in which he states that his 'first time' was during a drunken incestuous rendezvous with his mother in an outhouse. The Hustler parody portrays respondent and his mother as drunk and immoral, and suggests that respondent is a hypocrite who preaches only when he is drunk. In small print at the bottom of the page, the ad contains the disclaimer, 'ad parody—not to be taken seriously.' The magazine's table of contents also lists the ad as 'Fiction; Ad and Personality Parody.'" 485 U.S. at 48.

17. *Id.* at 49.

18. *Id.* at 56. All eight justices participating in the decision agreed with the result, but Justice White concurred only in the judgment, not the reasoning, of the majority.

19. *Id.* at 53.

20. 501 U.S. 663 (1991).

21. *Cohen v. Cowles Media Co.*, 457 N.W.2d 199 (Minn. 1990).

22. Cowles's claim here might be a case of "be careful what you wish for." A finding that the press could break promises with impunity would surely lead some sources to distrust a promise of confidentiality and decline to talk. And the press would be in the daunting but not impossible position of arguing that reporters are entitled to conceal the identity of confidential sources while also claiming that the press can break confidentiality promises whenever it deems the information newsworthy.

23. 501 U.S. at 669.

24. *Id.* at 671.

25. *Id.* at 675 n.3.

26. *Shulman v. Group W Productions, Inc.*, 955 P.2d 469, 495 (Cal. 1998).

27. *Sanders v. American Broadcasting Co.*, 978 P.2d 67, 77 (Cal. 1999).

28. 532 U.S. 514 (2001).

29. *Id.* at 517.

30. The Court assumed for purposes of the decision that the station had reason to know that the conversation was illegally intercepted. *Id.* at 525.

31. *Id.* at 535–536.

32. *Id.* at 536. "Strict scrutiny" is the Court's shorthand way of saying that any infringement on speech protected by the First Amendment

must serve a very strong state interest that cannot be satisfied in another way.

33. *Id.* at 537.

34. *Id.* at 538–539.

35. *Id.* at 539.

36. *Id.* at 540.

37. 501 U.S. at 678–679.

38. *Id.* at 678.

39. *Desnick v. American Broadcasting Co.*, 44 F.3d 1345 (7th Cir. 1995).

40. Compare what the *Chicago Sun-Times* did while investigating whether the police department "manipulated a homicide investigation" because of a suspect's political connections. It published information, unlawfully received, from motor vehicle department records, which by statute were confidential. It was sued for doing so. The court upheld the complaint. The "specific details [from the records] are largely cumulative of lawfully obtained information published in that very same article." The violation did "little to advance Sun-Times's reporting on a story of public concern." *Dahlstrom v. Sun-Times Media, LLC*, 777 F.3d 937, 953 (7th Cir. 2015).

41. I put aside the possibility that the speaker may not even have a claim based on the subterfuge because his office belongs to the state.

42. 44 F.3d at 1351.

43. *Id.* at 1352.

44. *Taus v. Loftus*, 151 P.3d 1185, 1221–1222 (Cal. 2007).

45. "Reporter Pleads Guilty in Theft of Voice Mail," *New York Times*, September 25, 1998.

46. *Le Mistral, Inc. v. Columbia Broadcasting System*, 402 N.Y.S.2d 815, 816–817 (1978), is instructive. A reporter, Lucille Rich, and a camera crew were told

to visit a number of restaurants which had been cited for health code violations by the Health Services Administration of New York City. Plaintiff restaurant was on the list. The camera crew and Ms. Rich entered the restaurant at approximately 2:00 p.m. with the camera working ("rolling"), which necessitated the utilization of bright lights for filming purposes. After entering the premises in this fashion, Ms. Rich and the camera crew were commanded to leave by plaintiff's president. It appears that these CBS employees were on the premises for a period of time during which the camera continued to roll. . . .

Initially, we are confronted with defendant CBS's claim that despite the tort committed, defendant is insulated from any damage award by virtue of the First Amendment to the United States Constitution. Clearly, the First Amendment is not a shibboleth before which all other rights must succumb.

The court affirmed the jury's award of $1,200 in compensatory damages but remanded for further proceedings on the $250,000 punitive-damage award.

47. In the Wyoming case, the National Press Photographers Association was among the plaintiffs.

48. *Animal Legal Defense Fund v. Otter*, 118 F.Supp.3d 1195 (D. Idaho 2015). The law (§18–7042) provides:

A person commits the crime of interference with agricultural production if the person knowingly:

(a) Is not employed by an agricultural production facility and enters an agricultural production facility by force, threat, misrepresentation or trespass;

(b) Obtains records of an agricultural production facility by force, threat, misrepresentation or trespass;

(c) Obtains employment with an agricultural production facility by force, threat, or misrepresentation with the intent to cause economic or other injury to the facility's operations . . . [or] business interest . . ."

(d) Enters an agricultural production facility that is not open to the public and, without the facility owner's express consent or pursuant to judicial process or statutory authorization, makes audio or video recordings of the conduct of an agricultural production facility's operations. . . .

49. 118 F.Supp.3d at 1203. The court cited the "Stolen Valor" case in the Supreme Court. The Court there invalidated a statute that made it a

crime falsely to claim receipt of military declarations or medals. *United States v. Alvarez*, 567 U.S.709 (2012).

50. 118 F.Supp.3d at 1204.
51. *Id.* at 1205.
52. *Id.* at 1207.
53. *Id.* at 1207.
54. *Animal Legal Defense Fund v. Wasden*, 878 F.3d 1184 (9th Cir. 2018).
55. *Id.* at 1203.
56. *Western Watersheds Project v. Michael*, 869 F.3d 1189, 1195 (10th Cir. 2017). The 2016 law amended a 2015 law after a preliminary ruling in the case went partly against the state.
57. *Id.* at 1196 (quoting *Sorrell v. IMS Health Inc.*, 564 U.S. 552, 570 (2011)).

6. FOUR LEGISLATIVE CHANGES TO SAFEGUARD INVESTIGATIVE REPORTING

1. Michael Bartel, Pew Research Center, "Newspapers Fact Sheet" (2017), http://www.journalism.org/fact-sheet/newspapers. These numbers are not adjusted for inflation.
2. Pew Research Center, "Newspaper Ad Revenue from Digital and Print" (2015), http://www.journalism.org/chart/newspaper-ad-revenue-from -digital-and-print/.
3. Robert Kaiser, "The Bad News About the News," Brookings Institution Essay, October 16, 2014.
4. ASNE, 2015 Census, http://asne.org/content.asp?pl=121&sl=415&con tentid=415.
5. Pew Research Center, Newspaper Fact Sheet (2017).
6. BLS, "Employment Trends in Newspaper Publishing and Other Media, 1990–2016," https://www.bls.gov/opub/ted/2016/employment -trends-in-newspaper-publishing-and-other-media-1990-2016.htm. In January 1990, the first month on the BLS chart, the number was 455,000. It fell nearly every month thereafter.
7. The Marshall Project is a "nonpartisan, nonprofit news organization that seeks to create and sustain a sense of national urgency about the U.S. criminal justice system. We achieve this through award-winning journalism, partnerships with other news outlets and public forums. In all of our work we strive to educate and enlarge the audience of

people who care about the state of criminal justice." https://www
.themarshallproject.org/about/. ProPublica's mission is "to expose
abuses of power and betrayals of the public trust by government,
business, and other institutions, using the moral force of investigative journalism to spur reform through the sustained spotlighting of
wrongdoing." https://www.propublica.org/about/.

8. There has been discussion of foundation investments (not grants) in
   low-profit limited-liability companies ("L3Cs"). About a dozen states
   recognize L3Cs. They are defined in a way that could make it possible
   for a foundation to invest in them without risk to the foundation's status. They are not nonprofit but low profit, so the investing foundation
   could eventually recoup its investment. The investment is thereby
   replenished for use another time. Essentially, the investment would
   be allowed because it would advance the foundation's purpose, which
   would also be the L3C's purpose, whereas otherwise the investment
   would be disallowed. Steven Chiodini and David Levitt, "Program-
   Related Investing in L3Cs: A Question-and-Answer Guide," *Journal
   of Taxation* 41 (January 2013). So far, the idea does not seem to have
   caught on.

9. The IRS website makes this quite clear: "Under the Internal Revenue
   Code, all section 501(c)(3) organizations are absolutely prohibited
   from directly or indirectly participating in, or intervening in, any
   political campaign on behalf of (or in opposition to) any candidate for
   elective public office. Contributions to political campaign funds or
   public statements of position (verbal or written) made on behalf of the
   organization in favor of or in opposition to any candidate for public
   office clearly violate the prohibition against political campaign activity. Violating this prohibition may result in denial or revocation of
   tax-exempt status and the imposition of certain excise taxes." https://
   www.irs.gov/charities-non-profits/charitable-organizations/the
   -restriction-of-political-campaign-intervention-by-section-501c3-tax
   -exempt-organizations.

10. David Schizer cites this option in his paper "Subsidizing the Press,"
    Journal of Legal Analysis 3, no. 1 (2011).

11. A tax-exempt organization is required "to pay income tax when the organi-
    zation regularly carries on a trade or business that is not substantially

related to the organization's exempt purposes." "Does My Nonprofit Need to Pay Tax? Understanding Unrelated Business Income Tax," *Nonprofit Quarterly* (2011), https://nonprofitquarterly.org/2011/12/25/does-my-nonprofit-need-to-pay-tax-understanding-unrelated-business-income-tax/.

12. Funds might also be available to the low-profit limited-liability companies described in note 8.

13. Leonard Downie and Michael Schudson, "The Reconstruction of American Journalism," *Columbia Journalism Review* (2009).

14. *Id.*

15. For this proposal the authors cite the economists Dean Baker and Randy Baker. Robert McChesney and John Nichols, *The Death and Life of American Journalism* (New York: Nation Books, 2010), chap. 4.

16. McChesney and Nicols, *The Death and Life of American Journalism*.

17. Schizer cites the risk to independence in "Subsidizing the Press," 53–55.

18. The president's ability to fire agency heads without cause will depend on the statutory language and the nature of the position. But if Congress makes it clear that termination may only be for cause, termination requires proof of "inefficiency, neglect of duty, or malfeasance in office." *Humphrey's Ex'r v. United States*, 295 U.S. 602, 621–624 (1935). An allegation of cause must be proved because "*all* officers protected by a for-cause removal provision and later subject to termination are entitled to 'notice and [a] hearing' in the 'courts,' as without such review 'the appointing power' otherwise 'could remove at pleasure or for such cause as [only] it deemed sufficient.'" *Free Enterprise Fund v. Accounting Oversight Board*, 561 U.S. 477, 536 (2010) (Breyer, J. dissenting), quoting *Reagan v. United States*, 182 U.S. 419, 425 (1901). See, generally, Adrian Vermeule, "Conventions of Agency Independence," *Columbia Law Review* 113 (2013): 1163.

19. The Inspector General Act of 1978 as amended provides in part:

> (a) There shall be at the head of each Office an Inspector General who shall be appointed by the President, by and with the advice and consent of the Senate, without regard to political

affiliation and solely on the basis of integrity and demonstrated ability in accounting, auditing, financial analysis, law, management analysis, public administration, or investigations. Each Inspector General shall report to and be under the general supervision of the head of the establishment involved. . . . Neither the head of the establishment nor the officer next in rank below such head shall prevent or prohibit the Inspector General from initiating, carrying out, or completing any audit or investigation, or from issuing any subpoena during the course of any audit or investigation.

(b) An Inspector General may be removed from office by the President. If an Inspector General is removed from office or is transferred to another position or location within an establishment, the President shall communicate in writing the reasons for any such removal or transfer to both Houses of Congress, not later than 30 days before the removal or transfer. . . .

20. I recognize the risk that private donors to organizations that support investigative reporting may take their money elsewhere if the government appropriates funds. I do not think this is a big risk. The government's largesse will leave many gaps. Government funding for the arts and education occurs alongside private contributions to museums, nonprofit theater companies, and colleges.

21. Seth Lipsky, "All the News That's Fit to Subsidize," *Wall Street Journal*, October 21, 2009.

22. Schizer, "Subsidizing the Press," 54.

23. *Id.* at 54–55.

24. *Id.* at 54.

25. See Lipsky, "All the News That's Fit to Subsidize."

26. *Brooklyn Institute of Arts and Sciences v. City of New York*, 64 F.Supp.2d 184 (E.D.N.Y. 1999).

27. John Coffee, "Market Failure and the Economic Case for a Mandatory Disclosure System," *Virginia Law Review* 70 (1984): 717, 725. A footnote states: "Technically, a public good is characterized by both nonexcludability and indivisibility—the latter term meaning that use or consumption of the good by one user does not diminish it for

others. Thus, once a public park is built, it is infeasible to exclude citizens who did not contribute taxes or contributions toward its construction. Moreover, such citizens' use of the park does not diminish its availability to others."

28. 376 U.S. 254, 270 (1964).
29. 372 U.S. 335, 344 (1963).
30. *Argersinger v. Hamlin*, 407 U.S. 25, 37 (1972).
31. *Ake v. Oklahoma*, 470 U.S. 68, 83 (1985). In 2017, the Court overturned a death sentence because although Alabama may have provided the defense with a psychiatric examination of the defendant, it did not help "the defense evaluate [the psychiatrist's] report or [the defendant's] extensive medical records and translate these data into a legal strategy," as *Ake* required. Nor did it provide the other assistance *Ake* required. *McWilliams v. Dunn*, 137 S.Ct. 1790 (2017).
32. 20 U.S.C. §951(4).
33. 20 U.S.C. §956(b).
34. 20 U.S.C. §957(b).
35. *Id.*
36. 20 U.S.C. §953(c).
37. In time, grants might also become available to low-profit limited-liability companies, described in note 8.
38. The endowment will have to find the proper balance between transparency and confidentiality. The presumption should be in favor of transparency. The endowment should be subject to the FOIA. However, confidentiality may be necessary for some funding requests, at least until the work is completed.
39. The Trump administration's proposed budget for FY 2018 would reduce that to $42 million to be used "for the orderly closure of the agency." "NEH Statement on Proposed FY 2018 Budget," https://www.neh.gov/news/press-release/2017-05-23.
40. John Smith, "Sheldon Adelson, the Billionaire Who Bankrupted Me," *Daily Beast*, February 2, 2013. Adelson has also sued a *Wall Street Journal* reporter who was a co-byline on a story that described him as "foul-mouthed." The suit was filed in Hong Kong. Adelson did not name the *Journal* or the other writer. That case settled in 2017, with each side paying its own lawyers and no money changing hands.

The offending article remains online. Lukas Alpert, "Libel Lawsuit Settled Between Casino Magnate Sheldon Adelson, *WSJ* Reporter," *Wall Street Journal*, January 12, 2017.

41. *Trump v. O'Brien*, 958 A.2d 85 (N.J. App. 2008).
42. *Trump v. O'Brien*, 29 A.3d 1090 (N.J. App. 2011). The lawsuit was filed in January 2006. The final appellate decision dismissing is dated September 7, 2011. See also Ian Tuttle, "The Litigious—and Bullying—Mr. Trump," *National Review*, February 19, 2016, http://www.nationalreview.com/article/431575/donald-trump-tim-obrien-courtroom-story.
43. Restatement of Torts (Second) §675.
44. Reporters Committee for Freedom of the Press, "Chart: Anti-SLAPP Laws and Journalists," https://www.rcfp.org/slapp-stick-fighting-frivolous-lawsuits-against-journalists/chart-anti-slapp-laws-and-journalists.
45. California Code of Civil Procedure, section 425.16(e).
46. *Id.* at (b)(1).
47. *Id.* at (c)(1).
48. H.R. 2304.
49. Andrew Ross Sorkin, "Peter Thiel, Tech Billionaire, Reveals Secret War with *Gawker*," *New York Times*, May 25, 2016; Sydney Ember, "*Gawker* and Hulk Hogan Reach $31 Million Settlement," *New York Times*, November 2, 2016; Peter Sterne, "Gawker Media Files for Bankruptcy," Politico, June 10, 2016 (*Gawker* could not post $50 million appeal bond).
50. Nick Madigan, "Jury Tacks on $25 Million to *Gawker*'s Bill in the Hulk Hogan Case," *New York Times*, March 21, 2016.
51. 5 U.S.C. §552(a)(4)(A)(iii).
52. 5 U.S.C. §552(a)(6)(E)(v)(II) (emphasis added).
53. 5 U.S.C. §552(a)(6)(E)(i) provides:

> Each agency shall promulgate regulations . . . providing for expedited processing of requests for records—
>> (I) in cases in which the person requesting the records demonstrates a compelling need; and
>> (II) in other cases determined by the agency.

54. 28 C.F.R. §16.5(e) provides: "(1) Requests and appeals shall be processed on an expedited basis whenever it is determined that they involve:

    (i) Circumstances in which the lack of expedited processing could reasonably be expected to pose an imminent threat to the life or physical safety of an individual;

    (ii) An urgency to inform the public about an actual or alleged Federal Government activity, if made by a person who is primarily engaged in disseminating information;

    (iii) The loss of substantial due process rights; or

    (iv) A matter of widespread and exceptional media interest in which there exist possible questions about the government's integrity that affect public confidence."

55. *Al-Fayed v. CIA*, 254 F.3d 300, 310 (D.C. Cir. 2001).

56. *Tripp v. Department of Defense*, 193 F. Supp. 2d 229, 241 (D.D.C. 2002).

57. "Department of Justice Guide to the Freedom of Information Act: Procedural Requirements," 36–37, https://www.justice.gov/oip/doj -guide-freedom-information-act-0.

58. 32 C.F.R. §701.8(f)(5). The Defense Department further explains: "Compelling need also means that the information is urgently needed by an individual primarily engaged in disseminating information in order to inform the public concerning actual or alleged Federal Government activity. An individual primarily engaged in disseminating information means a person whose primary activity involves publishing or otherwise disseminating information to the public. Representatives of the news media would normally qualify as individuals primarily engaged in disseminating information. Other persons must demonstrate that their primary activity involves publishing or otherwise disseminating information to the public."

59. 5 U.S.C. §552(a)(6)(E)(ii)(II).

60. *Id.* at §552(a)(6)(E)(iii).

61. A court's own rules may do so.

62. See, e.g., *Detroit Free Press, Inc. v. Department of Justice*, 73 F.3d 93, 98 (6th Cir. 1996): "In determining whether a prevailing FOIA complainant should be awarded attorneys' fees, a district court should consider at least the following factors: 'the benefit to the public

deriving from the case; the commercial benefit to the complainant and the nature of its interest in the records; and whether the agency's withholding had a reasonable basis in law.'" After considering these factors, the lower court awarded the *Free Press* counsel fees and the circuit court affirmed even though "both parties to the dispute recognize that the issue before the court is one of first impression and that the position espoused by the Department of Justice is reasonable." An unrelated holding in the case was overruled twenty years later. *Detroit Free Press, Inc. v. Department of Justice*, 829 F.3d 478 (6th Cir. 2016).

63. Florida Statutes Annotated §119.12 (emphasis added).

64. 5 U.S.C. §552(a)(4)(E)(i) (emphasis added).

65. New York Public Officers Law §89.

66. *Blue v. Bureau of Prisons*, 570 F.2d 529, 533 (5th Cir. 1978) (bracketed numbers added). The court continued: "These criteria were eliminated in the final version adopted by Congress, but as the Conference Report explained, 'by eliminating these criteria, the conferees did not intend to make the award of attorney fees automatic or to preclude the courts, in exercising their discretion as to awarding such fees, to take into consideration such criteria.' Hence attorneys' fees under the FOIA were not to be awarded as a matter of course, as in civil rights cases; rather, a court could use the Senate's four criteria to circumscribe the conditions under which it would make such an award. As the Conference Report explained, these four criteria were only eliminated 'because the existing body of law on the award of attorney fees recognizes such factors,' so that 'a statement of the criteria may be too delimiting and is unnecessary.'"

67. The court wrote: "In short, the question of whether to award attorneys' fees is left to the sound discretion of the court, guided principally by the Senate's four criteria and, in addition, by any applicable criteria from the older body of equitable decisions on attorneys' fees. Clearly, however, the Senate's four criteria are the central guidelines for the award of attorneys' fees to a prevailing party under FOIA." *Id* at 533.

68. Report, Amending the Freedom of Information Act, accompanying S. 2543 (1974) at 169–170.

69. *Id.* at 171–172. "Newsmen," the Report stated, "would ordinarily recover fees even where the government's defense has a reasonable basis in law,

while corporate interests might recover where the withholding was without such basis."

70. *Long v. Internal Revenue Service*, 932 F.2d 1309, 1316 (9th Cir. 1991).

71. "Department of Justice Guide to the Freedom of Information Act: Attorney Fees," 27–28 (emphasis added). The department quotes *Frydman v. Department of Justice*, 852 F.Supp. 1497, 1504 (D. Kan. 1994): "Although the government did not offer case authority to support its position regarding the [records], we believe the government's position had a colorable basis. There is little, if any, case authority which directly holds contrary to the government's position."

72. 5 U.S.C. §552(a)(4)(A)(ii).

73. *Id.* The definition continues: "A publication contract would present a solid basis for such an expectation; the Government may also consider the past publication record of the requester in making such a determination."

74. See, e.g., *Bond v. Stanton*, 630 F.2d 1231, 1234 (7th Cir. 1980): "It is equally clear that defendants' good or bad faith is irrelevant under the [Civil Rights] Act."

75. *Fox v. Vice*, 563 U.S. 826, 833 (2011) (internal quotes omitted).

IN CONCLUSION: POTTER STEWART'S TRUTH

1. Potter Stewart, "Or of the Press," *Hastings Law Journal* 50 (1999): 705. Stewart worked in journalism in college. He spent two summers at a Cincinnati newspaper and was chairman of the *Yale Daily News*, according to his *New York Times* obituary, December 8, 1985.

2. Stewart, "Or of the Press," 707.

3. The focus on "the Executive Branch of the Federal Government" is explained by events at the time of the speech. It should not be interpreted as a limitation on the press's adversary role.

4. Stewart, "Or of the Press," 705.

5. *Id.*

6. *Id.*

7. Art Swift, "In U.S., Confidence in Newspapers Still Low but Rising," *Gallup*, 2017, http://news.gallup.com/poll/212852/confidence-news papers-low-rising.aspx.

8. Michael Barthel and Amy Mitchell, "Americans' Attitudes About the News Media Deeply Divided Along Partisan Lines," Pew Research Center, 2017, http://www.journalism.org/2017/05/10/americans-attitudes-about-the-news-media-deeply-divided-along-partisan-lines/.

9. *Food Lion, Inc. v. ABC/Capital Cities, Inc.*, 194 F.3d 505, 511 (4th Cir. 1999).

10. A dissent would have upheld the finding of fraud and the reduced punitive damages.

INDEX

234 INDEX

Internal Revenue Service (IRS),
150, 218n9
intrusion: as legal concept, 118–120;
newsgathering exception for,
126; newsworthiness and,
129–131, 136, 138, 140–142, 208n3
investigative journalism/reporting:
definition of, 6, 15; on food
safety, 144; journalist's privilege
in, 57–58; Press Clause and,
37–40; protections for, 6–7,
83–84; public apathy and, 40–42;
as public good, 157–159, 220n27;
Pulitzer Prize for, 7; time/
money required for, 42–43.
See also government funding, for
investigative reporting; money,
for journalism
investigative stories: challenges to,
40, 42; financial impediment to,
16; journals of opinion and, 90;
legal impediments to, 39
Iraq, invasion of/war in, 8, 106

jail, threat of, 27, 94–95, 115, 198n61,
201n23. *See also* prisons, access to
Janklow, William, 76–77, 204n20
Janklow v. Newsweek, Inc.,
204–205n22
Jones, RonNell Andersen,
201n23–4
journalism. *See* investigative
journalism/reporting
journalistic ethics, 70. *See also*
editorial judgment
journalists: "covered journalist,"
61–63, 202n24; definition of,

3–4; freelance, 59, 183;
"journalist's exception," 141; role
of, 43–46; secrets revealed by, 6;
threats to jail, 27, 94–95, 115,
198n61, 201n23. *See also* qualified
reporter's privilege/protection;
reporters
journals of opinion, 90
judicial deference, 4, 68. *See also*
deference to editors
Jungle, The (Sinclair), 144
Justice Department, 94, 106,
111–112, 175, 181

Kennedy, Anthony, 24–26, 35–36,
194n26, 194n32
KQED, Inc., Houchins v., 102, 104

Laker, Barbara, 7
*Landmark Communications, Inc. v.
Virginia*, 39
Lando, Herbert v., 195n43
"leak" cases/investigations, 96,
106–108, 110–111, 126, 129, 135,
161
Legacy of Suppression (Levy), 13
Lemann, Nicholas, 74–75, 203n15,
204n16
*Le Mistral, Inc. v. Columbia
Broadcasting System*, 215–216n46
Levy, Leonard, 13–14
liability, theory of, 129
libel: editorial judgment and, 4–5,
69, 204n22; as public concern/
interest, 194n26, 196n47;
standards applicable to,
195–196n43. *See also Cohen v.*

Rehnquist, William, 96, 124
religion, 16–17, 31, 47–49, 51
reporters: subpoenas to, 92–98,
  100–101, 104–112; threats to jail,
  27, 94–95, 115, 198n61, 201n23.
  See also journalists
reportorial judgement, 82. *See also*
  editorial judgment
reputational harm, 128, 168
Restatement of the Law of Torts,
  117–119, 203n9, 213n4
Reynolds, Andrea, 54–56
Rhodes, Williams v., 193n15
Rich, Lucille, 215–216n46
Richmond Newspapers, Inc. v.
  Virginia, 213n3
right to counsel, 161, 185
Risen, James, 94, 106, 109–111,
  211n37
Robert Welch, Inc., Gertz v., 195n43,
  196n47
Ross v. Midwest Communications,
  Inc., 203n9
Ruderman, Wendy, 7
Rule 501 (Federal Rules of
  Evidence), 113
Russian influence, in US elections,
  158

Sanders, Mark, 130
Sanders v. American Broadcasting
  Co., 214n27
Saxbe v. Washington Post Co., 101,
  103
Scalia, Antonin, 25, 194n26
Schizer, David, 155
Schmidt, Benno, 197–198n61

Schudson, Michael, 16, 152–153, 155
Second Circuit Court of Appeals,
  54–57
self-incrimination, privilege
  against, 100, 185
Sentelle, David B., 107
Serrano, Andres, 155
Seventh Circuit Court of Appeals
  (Chicago), 105
shield laws, 52, 59–60, 62, 105,
  111–112, 167, 183, 200–201n21,
  202n23
Shoen v. Shoen, 57
Shulman v. Group W. Productions,
  Inc., 203n6, 214n26–27
Sinclair, Upton, 58, 144
SLAPP (strategic lawsuits against
  public participation): features
  of, 169–171; press protection
  and, 168–169; at state/federal
  level, 9, 147
Snowden, Edward, 82
Society of Professional Journalists,
  69, 90, 201n23, 202n2
sources. *See* confidential sources
Souter, David, 5, 128–129, 132,
  134–137
South Dakota, 76–77
Speech Clause: editorial judgment
  and, 5, 82–83; independent role
  for, 13; meaning of, 5; Press
  Clause redundancy and, 18,
  21–22; press freedoms and,
  45–46; protections of, 3–4, 17, 20,
  37, 67; reliance on, 33; Supreme
  Court treatment of, 11; violation
  of, 145